GLOBAL AMPLIFERS

Global Amplifers

*Strategies to
Think and Act
Bigger
in a Changing
World*

SOPHIE KRANTZ

Sophie Krantz

CONTENTS

SECTION 'THEM': EXTERNAL INFLUENCES AND MARKET POSITION

SECTION 'IT': ENABLING TECHNOLOGY

SECTION 'TOGETHER': COLLECTIVE SUCCESS AND COMMUNITY

CONCLUSION

RULE THE WORLD

Published by Sophie Krantz
First published in 2024 in Melbourne, Australia
Copyright © 2024 by Sophie Krantz
www.sophiekrantz.com
ISBN 978-1-7635976-1-7 (paperback)
ISBN 978-1-7635976-0-0 (ebook)
The moral rights of the author have been asserted.

To the reader ready to expand their horizons: may you find growth and success in a wider world of opportunity.

INTRODUCTION

I used to ask people, "What's your dream job?" This question often appealed to those aspiring to achieve more.

Now, my question has evolved to, "What do you want to be the best in the world at?"

The job question places individuals within the confines of an organisation, bound by its rules and limits on their potential. It embeds them into a system where autonomy is often compromised.

The second question challenges us to see beyond the hurdles of corporate resistance, stakeholder pushback, and social judgement. It involves looking at what matters most to us and how we could leverage this drive to achieve next-level success. It's a difficult question, but it encourages us to think expansively. Being the best isn't about status or wielding power for personal gain but about driving necessary progress. By contemplating scenarios like ending conflicts, investing in sustainable technologies, or leading global dialogues, we start to see the impact of vast, benevolent influence.

What if you could:

- End wars across continents?
- Accelerate the shift from fossil fuels?
- Facilitate crucial conversations among global leaders?
- Foresee and mitigate massive socio-economic and environmental crises?
- Drive initiatives that tackle global social inequalities within five years?

These considerations push us to envision and strive for a better world, guiding us toward actions that have a meaningful impact.

This book is written with the intent to expand your leadership through connectivity. It introduces 24 Global Amplifiers — practical tools designed to enhance your leadership capabilities beyond conventional limits. Accessible to anyone with an internet connection, curiosity, and a readiness to step out of their comfort zone, these strategies help you discover insights, gain understanding, and apply knowledge in impactful ways.

Global Amplifiers is a guide for applying your ambitions where they can make a difference where it matters most to you.

GLOBAL AMPLIFIERS: STRATEGIES TO THINK AND ACT BIGGER IN A CHANGING WORLD

	Why	What	How	Who	When	What's Next?
Together	19 Aim For The Moon To Maximise Breakthroughs	20 Question The Value Established Powers & Intermediaries	21 Aim Big To Unlock Potential (10x Versus 10%)	22 Confirm Your Dedicated Audience To Co-Design With (1000 True Fans)	23 Embrace Diversity Of Thought & Culture To Lead Globally	24 Ask: What If You Were The Globally Dominant Player?
It (Enabling Technology)	13 Embrace The Ease Of Expanding Your Worldview	14 Build On Local Success For Global Results	15 Harness Digital Tools To Connect & Collaborate Globally	16 Build Strategic Connections For Global Reach	17 Leverage Insight & Learning With AI	18 Design For One World, Diminishing Borders & Barriers
Them	7 Surpass The Limits Set By Others' Achievements	8 Confirm The Problem You Solve & Where Does It Exists in the World	9 The World's Unmet Needs Contain Your Biggest Commercial Opportunity	10 Know Your Current & Emerging Competition	11 Tap into 5.55 Billion Active Internet Users	12 Break The Mould Of Traditional Pathways To Success
You	1 Define Ambition On Your Terms, Not On The Expectations Of Others	2 Focus On What You The Best At In The World	3 Leverage Your Underlying Talents, Assets, Network, & Influence	4 Determine Who Supports Your Boldest Goals	5 Redefine Your Niche; Zoom-Out, To Zero-In	6 Imagine If You Were To Start Again

Why Global Amplifiers?

I wrote this book because too many brilliant and high-performing individuals aren't reaching their full potential. Restrictive societal, cultural, and organisational norms often trap them in a game they can't win.

Yet, the world needs these people to win. We need the brightest minds to tackle global challenges, revolutionise business practices, and lead organisations, institutions, cities and nations towards peace and prosperity.

The world is rapidly changing. We now live in a highly interconnected digital era where geographical boundaries don't restrict our actions or cap our achievements.

As a global strategist and an Exponential Organizations (ExOs) practitioner, I have worked with leadership teams worldwide. My experience has shown that small, focused actions can drive significant change and achieve ambitious goals. Whether through ten-week innovation sprints or strategy design programmes, I've seen teams transform their mindsets and capabilities, proving that even selective use of the 24 Global Amplifiers can open vast commercial and growth possibilities.

This book draws on extensive global projects and my journey of personal and professional evolution. It's designed to transform your curiosity into action and help you build meaningful global connections.

In today's volatile corporate world, success might seem elusive. However, the interconnectedness of our digital world offers unprecedented opportunities. The 24 Global Amplifiers provide practical, impactful strategies that can revolutionise your approach and elevate your success.

This book is more than about setting goals; it challenges you to broaden your ambitions, make decisive choices, and implement significant changes effectively. It encourages you to rethink your potential and embrace a wider perspective on what you can achieve.

What's an Interconnected World?

An interconnected world in the digital age is a space where technology connects us to vast information and diverse cultures, economies, and communities worldwide. It makes geographical distances and time zones irrelevant to communication, collaboration, and commerce. In this environment, individuals and organisations use digital networks to enhance learning, create business opportunities, and build relationships across borders.

This connectivity offers instant access to a global audience, enabling the swift and efficient exchange of ideas, goods, and services. It transforms societal norms, business practices, and personal interactions, driving innovation and creating opportunities for growth in all aspects of life.

This book guides you in navigating this interconnected world. It shows how to use digital capabilities to achieve personal and professional goals in a setting where adaptability, cultural understanding, and technological proficiency are key.

In the digital era, our decisions and strategies are influenced by global trends, technologies, talent, competitors, customers, communities, capital, and regulations. Success in leadership means going beyond simple market penetration; it requires envisioning and achieving an elevated position, deploying effective frameworks and models to reach ambitious goals.

Who Is This Book For?

This book is designed for current and aspiring leaders who aim to surpass conventional success. It is ideal for those who recognize that traditional approaches and mere conformity are insufficient in today's interconnected, innovative world.

This practical guide supports those challenging the status quo and leading significant changes, whether they are startup founders disrupting markets, corporate executives driving innovation, or professionals building influential global networks. It provides the strategies and insights needed to broaden your influence and achieve your goals.

The book is particularly valuable for leaders who appreciate the power of digital connectivity and are eager to explore innovative ways of thinking and acting for business success.

This publication emphasises the need for an expansive vision and strategic use of digital technology, aligning with the World Economic Forum's insights in their report, 'Putting Skills First: Opportunities for Building Efficient and Equitable Labour Markets'. The January 2024 report stresses a skills-first approach to addressing talent gaps and improving labour market efficiency, advocating for innovative hiring practices that prioritise skills over formal qualifications and urging companies to adapt to rapid technological and environmental changes.

Aligned with the World Economic Forum's recommendations, this book acts as a practical toolkit for navigating the global economy. It emphasises innovative recruitment and talent development strategies that prioritise diversity, inclusivity, and sustainability, preparing leaders to meet the dynamic demands of the global market and drive progress toward a more inclusive and sustainable future.

How To Use This Book

Global Amplifiers is designed to transform your approach to global business success. It features 24 pivotal statements guiding your leadership journey, challenging you to rethink and redefine your potential.

At its core, this book champions the transformative power of ambition and agency. It's about shifting from simply aspiring to be better to fundamentally redefining excellence. Each chapter poses probing questions about your business and personal motivations, inspired by Steve Blank's insight: "There are no facts inside your building, so get outside." These questions encourage you to explore beyond your immediate environment and conventional thinking.

The structure is thematic:

'**You**' delves into personal ambition and success, urging you to define these on your terms and explore the support systems that bolster your goals.

'**Them**' shifts the focus externally, challenging you to surpass existing achievements and understand the unique challenges your business addresses.

'**It**' examines technology's role in expanding your reach, emphasising the importance of digital tools in achieving local and global impact.

'**Together**' looks at collective success and reevaluates partnerships and industry standards, aiming for breakthroughs that redefine markets.

'**Who**' encourages building a community aligned with your vision, identifying key people and strategic connections that extend your influence.

'**When**' emphasises timing, stressing the importance of seizing moments that enhance diversity of thought and broaden engagement.

'**What's Next?**' inspires thoughts on future leadership and the impact of starting anew, pushing you to design a future without boundaries.

Each of the 24 Global Amplifiers comes with five reflective questions, turning reading into an interactive experience. This non-linear structure serves as a web of inquiry, allowing you to navigate the content in a way that best suits your needs.

'Global Amplifiers' acts as a strategic partner in your leadership development, prompting you to think differently and achieve unprecedented success. As you engage with each chapter, use the questions to deepen your understanding and expand your leadership acumen.

Let this book amplify your ambitions, guiding you to master leadership in an interconnected, evolving world.

SECTION 'YOU': PERSONAL AMBITION AND IDENTITY

This section is the foundation of your journey, where you examine the internal drivers of your success. It invites introspection on how you perceive and define your own ambition, separate from external expectations. By questioning the core of your motivation and the identity you carve out in your professional landscape, 'You' establishes the groundwork for authentic growth. It encourages you to assess who is in your corner, championing your vision, and to determine the moments that call for a strategic pivot in your approach. Here, you'll align your personal values with your professional aspirations, setting a course for success that is uniquely yours.

Global Amplifier 1. Define Ambition On Your Terms, Not On The Expectations of Others

"To live is to choose. But to choose well, you must know who you are and what you stand for, where you want to go and why you want to get there." - Kofi Annan

Ambition is often viewed negatively, yet it serves as a vital driving force for a range of successful people including sporting stars, business leaders, and politicians. It can act as a catalyst for personal achievements and pioneering industry innovations. Recognising the positive role of ambition can inspire us to attain greater success than we might otherwise achieve.

Setting a course for ambition on your own terms, rather than succumbing to external pressures, is crucial in forging a path that is truly yours. It involves choosing a unique path over the conventional one, guided by your values, interests, and the impact you aim to create. When fueled by intrinsic motivation, ambition not only propels you forward but also sustains you through inevitable challenges.

Our perceptions of success are profoundly shaped by societal norms. From a young age, we are inundated with messages dictating the criteria for success. These societal standards become deeply embedded, influencing our ambitions subconsciously. Acknowledging and disentangling from these external influences is vital to pursuing a concept of success that aligns with our personal values.

The stories of Sara Blakely and Richard Branson demonstrate the heights that can be reached when ambition is defined on one's own terms.

Sara Blakely's journey to founding Spanx is a quintessential story of innovation born out of personal need and acute market observation. Her ambition was ignited by her own experience and a simple question: Why didn't shapewear that didn't compromise comfort exist? Blakely, then selling fax machines door-to-door, used her life savings of $5,000 to answer this question. She took a leap into an industry she had no experience in, armed with nothing but a prototype and a patent application she wrote herself. Her ambition was rooted in the belief that she could create something for women like herself, something that wasn't available in the market.

What set Blakely apart was her hands-on approach and relentless determination. She personally visited mills, pitched her idea to hosiery companies, and even demonstrated her product in the ladies' restroom to a Neiman Marcus buyer, which led to her first major order. Her approach to business was unconventional, but it was this unique vision that disrupted the fashion and retail industry. Spanx became a cultural phenomenon, not just for its products but for its brand ethos that championed women's comfort and confidence.

Richard Branson's journey is similarly marked by a distinct personal vision. Starting with a magazine named 'Student' at the age of 16, he went on to create a brand that is a byword for innovation and customer service – the Virgin Group. Branson's ventures span music, airlines, telecommunications, and even space travel with Virgin Galactic. His entrepreneurial spirit is driven by the philosophy of "Oh, screw it, let's do it," showcasing his appetite for risk-taking and breaking the mould. Each of Virgin's companies began as a solution to a problem or a better alternative to what was available, echoing Branson's personal mission to improve people's lives.

Branson's strategy often involved entering well-established markets and turning them on their heads, be it through Virgin Atlantic's unprecedented in-flight entertainment and customer service or Virgin Mobile's shake-up of the mobile phone industry. His success builds on his belief that business should be fun, challenging, and a force for good.

Both Blakely and Branson share the trait of being undeterred by the lack of a traditional roadmap or the daunting prospect of entering industries where they were outsiders. Instead, they trusted in their vision, using their unique strengths to build companies that not only became leaders in their respective industries but also changed those sectors forever. Their stories are not just about the success of their companies but about the validation of their personal standards of ambition, which encouraged innovation, emphasised customer satisfaction, and valued disruptive thinking.

In defining ambition on your terms, you free yourself from the weight of external expectations, allowing for a pursuit of success that is more fulfilling and aligned with who you are. Such ambition is not just about reaching the pinnacles of success; it's about creating a legacy that resonates with your personal story and values.

Reflect upon your journey and consider these five questions to understand how your personal ambition can shape your success:

1. How have external expectations influenced my definition of success, and what steps can I take to redefine success on my own terms?
2. What unique strengths and passions do I possess that could redefine my professional trajectory, similar to how Sara Blakely used her insight to change the fashion industry?
3. In what ways can I challenge the status quo in my field, as Richard Branson has done in multiple industries, to pave a new path for myself and others?
4. How can I ensure that my ambitions are serving not just my professional goals but also contributing to my overall sense of purpose and personal fulfilment?

5. What would success look like if it were measured only by my standards and how can I start to shift my focus towards this internal benchmark in the coming year and beyond?

At a time where business narratives are often shaped by external factors, it becomes even more critical to anchor your ambitions in a foundation of personal belief and individual passion.

Global Amplifier 2. Focus On What Are You The Best At In The World

"Be so good they can't ignore you." – Steve Martin

Trying to figure out what you're the best at is about aiming for personal greatness and making an impact worldwide. It's a challenging task that combines knowing yourself well with the ambition to reach your highest potential. This isn't about being better than others but about finding what unique skills you have that make you stand out globally.

The first step is getting to grips with your own expertise. This means closely examining your abilities, talents, and what makes you unique professionally. You need to be thorough and truthful in this process, focusing on your strongest points, whether it's a natural talent for innovation, a technical skill like coding, or a personal strength such as understanding others' feelings.

In a global context, being the 'best in the world' means assessing how your talents can be of service to a larger community or cause. It's not about being at the top of a leaderboard but about finding where your skills meet the world's needs in a way that no one else can replicate.

Ambition to be the best can be a powerful motivator. It can guide your career trajectory and focus your development efforts.

Dr. Jane Goodall's story is a compelling illustration of this principle. Her ambition was rooted in a profound empathy for animals, which when coupled with her sharp observational skills, fuelled her pioneering research on chimpanzees. Goodall's approach was characterised by her relentless dedication and patience, which enabled her to observe behaviours in chimpanzees that had previously gone unnoticed. She spent countless hours in Gombe, meticulously documenting the social and family interactions of chimpanzees, revealing striking parallels between them and humans, such as the use of tools, complex emotional lives, and deep familial bonds.

But Goodall's ambition extended beyond the scientific contributions she made. Her findings catalysed a paradigm shift in how we understand our place in the animal kingdom and underscored the importance of preserving these primates and their habitats. Her work sparked a global conversation about conservation and animal welfare, leading to tangible changes in how these issues are addressed.

Furthermore, Goodall's ambition propelled her to become an advocate for the environment. She founded the Jane Goodall Institute, which supports wildlife research, conservation, and education programmes. Her programme, Roots & Shoots, which began in 1991, is now a global movement that empowers young people to tackle environmental, conservation, and humanitarian issues.

Goodall's influence also extends into policy-making. Her expertise and advocacy have helped shape international conservation strategies and legislation. She's a UN Messenger of Peace and has been involved in various United Nations programmes, contributing her voice and influence to shape more ethical and sustainable environmental policies.

Dr. Jane Goodall's ambition brought her personal fulfilment and recognition, but more importantly, it created a legacy of conservation, compassion, and change that continues to inspire and guide efforts around the world. Her story is a testament to the profound impact one person's ambition can have when it's aligned with a greater purpose.

Being the best in your world means striving for excellence in a way that creates ripple effects. It's about sustained impact and legacy, where your work continues to influence long after initial achievements.

Reflective questions to ponder:

1. What unique combination of skills and experiences do I possess that could position me as the best in my field, and how can I continue to refine these?
2. How can I measure my progress toward becoming the best in the world in a way that is both motivating and realistic?
3. Who are the trailblazers in my field, like Dr. Goodall, and what can I learn from their journey to apply to my own?
4. What gaps or needs in the world can my unique skill set address, and how can I take steps towards making that impact?
5. If I were to envision myself as the best in the world at something, what would that look like in daily practice, and how would it change my current approach to personal and professional development?

By grappling with these questions, you set yourself on a trajectory that is not just about personal accolades but about crafting a legacy that is felt across the globe. It's about aligning your personal best with the world's greatest needs and finding where they intersect to define your own version of world-class excellence.

Global Amplifier 3. Leverage Your Underlying Talents, Assets, Network, and Influence

"My humanity is bound up in yours, for we can only be human together."
- Desmond Tutu

Leveraging your underlying talents, assets, network, and influence involves a strategic approach to utilising what naturally sets you apart. These characteristics, often operating beneath the surface, are critical in navigating your path towards success and making meaningful contributions. Whether it's the skills that come to you as second nature, the relationships you've cultivated over time, or the influence you've garnered through your actions and integrity, each plays a pivotal role in shaping your journey.

Talents and Assets: Your inherent skills and personal assets are your unique offerings to the world. These could range from an exceptional creative vision to analytical prowess or even resilience in the face of challenges. Recognising these talents and deploying them deliberately across your ventures can exponentially increase your effectiveness and efficiency.

Network: Your network encompasses a broad spectrum of relationships, from professional connections to personal friendships. Each interaction within this network carries potential value and opportunity. The art lies in nurturing these connections with mutual benefit in mind, which in turn can open doors to new avenues and insights.

Influence: Influence often accumulates subtly over time, through consistent actions, expertise, and the value you provide to those around you. It's about the impact you have on others' thoughts, behaviours, and decisions. Cultivating this influence thoughtfully can enable you to lead initiatives, drive change, and inspire others more effectively.

British chef Jamie Oliver stands as a paragon of how individual talents and influence, when judiciously leveraged, can catalyse substantial societal impact. Oliver's journey from a chef to a global advocate for nutritional education is a testament to the power of using one's natural gifts and platform for the greater good. His informal and accessible approach to cooking, characterised by a focus on simplicity and wholesomeness, has not only endeared him to millions worldwide but also revolutionised how people perceive and engage with food.

Oliver's rise to prominence began in the late 1990s with his television show, "The Naked Chef," which emphasised the joy of cooking with fresh, simple ingredients. However, it was his passionate commitment to improving the nutritional standards of school meals in the UK that showcased the breadth of his influence. Through his 2005 campaign, "Feed Me Better," Oliver sought to draw attention to the dire state of school lunches and the consequential effects on children's health and learning. His campaign was marked by a pragmatic approach, using his culinary skills to demonstrate how schools could serve nutritious, appealing meals without significantly higher costs.

The impact of Oliver's advocacy was significant. It lead to a public outcry for reform and also prompted the UK government to allocate additional funding for school meals and to overhaul nutritional standards. Oliver's efforts have extended beyond the UK; he has become a global voice in the movement against obesity and poor nutrition.

Oliver's ability to translate his culinary talents and personal ethos into a broader advocacy platform demonstrates the potential for individual influence to drive meaningful change. His initiatives, including various television series, cookbooks, and the Jamie Oliver Food Foundation, underscore his commitment to empowering people to make better food choices. Through these initiatives, Oliver has utilised his platform not just for personal gain but as a tool for public education and health advocacy.

His work is as a powerful reminder that personal success and societal impact are not mutually exclusive. By aligning his talents with a cause he was passionate about, Jamie Oliver has not only carved a unique niche for himself in the culinary world but has also contributed significantly to the global discourse on food and nutrition.

Reflecting on Jamie Oliver's journey allows us to consider how our unique skills and positions of influence can effect change in the areas we are passionate about. It challenges us to look beyond our immediate surroundings and to envision the broader impact we can achieve when we leverage our talents for a cause greater than ourselves.

To maximise your potential through these intrinsic strengths, consider the following reflective questions:

1. What unique talents do I possess that differentiate me in my field or community, and how can I further develop and strategically apply these talents to amplify my contributions?
2. How can I more effectively leverage my network to foster collaborations, gain new perspectives, and uncover opportunities that align with my goals and values?
3. In what ways can I expand and cultivate my influence to advocate for issues I am passionate about or to lead change in my community or industry?
4. How do my talents, network, and influence interconnect, and how can I synergize them to create a more significant impact?
5. Reflecting on examples like Jamie Oliver, what steps can I take to transform my natural abilities and influence into actionable initiatives that drive positive change on a wider scale?

By exploring these questions, you are invited to delve deeper into understanding and utilising your innate strengths and connections. This introspection can illuminate paths to leverage your unique assets, enabling you to achieve your aspirations more effectively and leave a lasting imprint on the world around you.

Global Amplifier 4. Determine Who Supports Your Boldest Goals

"Set your life on fire. Seek those who fan your flames." - Rumi

Identifying and engaging with those who support your most ambitious goals is a crucial strategy in navigating the path to next-level success. It's about recognising the individuals and groups - whether they are family, friends, mentors, colleagues, or part of your broader professional network - who offer support in various forms. This support could range from emotional encouragement and moral backing to practical help and professional guidance. Understanding the diverse roles these supporters play and how they contribute to your journey is essential for leveraging their support effectively.

A strategic approach to nurturing these relationships involves open communication, actively seeking their advice, and showing appreciation for their support. This not only solidifies your existing networks but also opens up new avenues for growth and collaboration, significantly enriching your quest towards achieving your ambitions.

The role of supportive networks in achieving monumental success cannot be overstated, as seen through the professional journeys of Serena Williams and Melanie Perkins, who have reached the top of their respective fields with the backing of their close circles.

Serena Williams, a name synonymous with excellence in tennis, has often highlighted the significant support she received from her family throughout her career. From the very beginning, her sister Venus Williams and her father, who also served as her coach, played pivotal roles in her development as an athlete. It was their faith in her abilities that fortified Serena's resolve and ambition. Venus, not just a sibling but a formidable competitor and ally on the court, provided a unique blend of rivalry and support that spurred Serena to push her limits. Their father, Richard Williams, was the architect of their tennis careers, guiding them with a visionary coaching approach that was both rigorous and unconventional. This familial support system was instrumental in Serena overcoming the myriad challenges associated with ascending to the top of the world tennis hierarchy, showcasing the power of belief and encouragement from those closest to her.

In the world of technology and entrepreneurship, Melanie Perkins' story as the co-founder of Canva echoes the critical importance of support from co-founders and investors. When Perkins first envisioned Canva, it was a bold ambition to simplify graphic design for everyone, making it accessible and user-friendly. This vision, while compelling, required the conviction and backing of others to come to fruition. Her co-founders, Cameron Adams and Cliff Obrecht, shared her vision and complemented her skills, forming a formidable team that would navigate the early challenges of a startup. The early investors in Canva were not just providing capital but were placing a bet on Perkins' vision and the team's ability to execute it. Their support went beyond financial investment to include mentorship, industry connections, and strategic guidance. This collective belief in Perkins' idea was a cornerstone in Canva's journey from a fledgling startup to a global platform.

These narratives confirm that behind individual success often lies a network of supporters who believe in the person's potential. Whether it's the unconditional support of a family, as in Serena Williams' case, or the strategic backing of co-founders and investors, like Melanie Perkins experienced, these supportive relationships are crucial. They provide not just the resources needed to pursue ambitious goals but also the emotional and motivational fuel to persist through challenges. The stories of Williams and Perkins illustrate how supportive networks function as a catalyst, transforming bold ambitions into tangible realities and demonstrating that while talent is critical, the journey to the top is seldom a solo endeavour.

However, the journey towards ambitious goals isn't always smooth, and the absence of a supportive network can pose significant challenges. A lack of encouragement, guidance, or validation can dampen motivation, diminish confidence, and hinder progress towards achieving potential milestones. Recognising and addressing this gap is critical for those who find themselves without adequate support.

In such situations, it becomes imperative to proactively seek out individuals or groups that align with your aspirations - be it through finding mentors who share your vision, joining communities that foster supportive environments, or exploring alternative sources of inspiration and encouragement.

Reflective questions to consider:

1. Who in my circle actively supports my boldest ambitions, and what specific roles do they play in my journey towards achieving these goals?
2. How can I more effectively engage with and show appreciation for my supporters to strengthen our relationship and ensure on-going support?
3. In areas where I feel a lack of support, what proactive steps can I take to identify and connect with potential mentors, communities, or networks that align with my aspirations?
4. What criteria should I consider when seeking out new supporters or mentors to ensure their guidance and support align with my objectives and values?
5. Reflecting on the examples of Serena Williams and Melanie Perkins, how can I leverage the support of my network to overcome challenges and accelerate my progress towards achieving my boldest goals?

By thoughtfully addressing these questions, you can strategise on effectively building and utilising a support system that not only backs your ambitions but also plays an integral role in your journey towards success.

Global Amplifier 5. Redefine Your Niche; Zoom-Out, To Zero-In

"The world is a complex place, and it's only by simplifying it that we can make sense of it." - Hans Rosling

Redefining your niche through a 'zoom-out, zero-in' approach is a strategic necessity in today's rapidly evolving market landscape. It allows for a recalibration of focus and objectives, ensuring that your efforts remain relevant, impactful, and aligned with the broader trends affecting your industry. This process is essential for staying ahead in a competitive environment, enabling you to seize new opportunities and address challenges proactively.

The 'zoom-out' phase involves stepping back to gain a comprehensive view of the external environment, including market dynamics, consumer behaviours, technological advancements, and socio-economic trends. This broad perspective is crucial for identifying potential shifts that could impact your niche, offering insights into where the market is heading and unveiling new avenues for growth.

Following this, the 'zero-in' phase requires a focused analysis of how these broader trends can be applied or adapted to your specific context. This might mean refining your product offerings, targeting a new customer segment, or incorporating innovative technologies into your business model or operations. The goal is to ensure that your niche remains dynamic and responsive to the changing landscape, thereby enhancing your competitive edge.

The Farm-to-Table Movement and the shift towards sustainable fashion are examples of how industries can evolve to meet changing consumer preferences through the strategic 'zoom-out, zero-in' approach, redefining their niches in the process.

The Farm-to-Table Movement represents a shift in the culinary world, where chefs and restaurateurs have broadened their culinary approaches to emphasise sustainability and local sourcing. This movement is rooted in the principle of sourcing ingredients directly from local farms and producers, thereby reducing the carbon footprint associated with long-distance food transportation and supporting local economies. By 'zooming out', these culinary professionals observed a growing consumer demand for meals that are not only delicious but also ethically sourced and environmentally friendly.

'Zeroing-in', they implemented this broader understanding into their menu planning and restaurant operations, offering dishes made with seasonal, locally sourced ingredients. This approach has enabled restaurants to provide fresher, more flavorful meals, tell the story of the food's origin, and create a connection between the diner, their food, and the local community. As a result, establishments embracing the Farm-to-Table philosophy have distinguished themselves in a saturated market, attracting diners who value transparency, sustainability, and quality in their dining experiences.

In the fashion industry, the shift towards sustainable fashion reflects a similar trajectory. As awareness of the environmental and ethical implications of fashion production has grown, consumer preferences have increasingly leaned towards brands that prioritise sustainability. Recognising this shift ('zooming-out'), fashion brands have started to realign their business practices ('zeroing-in') to cater to this new consumer ethos.

Adopting eco-friendly materials such as organic cotton, bamboo, recycled fabrics, and ethical production methods, these brands are addressing the environmental impact of the fashion industry. This strategic realignment involves changes in the materials used and also a reevaluation of the entire supply chain, from sourcing to production to distribution. By doing so, these brands are reducing their ecological footprint and also meeting the demand for fashion that consumers can feel good about supporting.

Both the Farm-to-Table Movement and sustainable fashion illustrate how industries can respond to changing consumer values by redefining their niches. This strategic adjustment requires a broad understanding of societal trends and a focused application of these insights to create offerings that resonate with contemporary consumers. In doing so, businesses not only ensure their relevance but also contribute positively to social and environmental well-being.

Engaging in this strategic exercise of redefining your niche is not a one-time task but an ongoing process. It's about continuously scanning the horizon for signals of change and being ready respond to emerging trends and opportunities.

Reflective questions to guide this process include:

1. How can I systematically 'zoom-out' to identify emerging trends and shifts in consumer preferences that may impact my current niche?
2. In what ways can I 'zero-in' to apply these broader insights to my specific area of expertise, ensuring my offerings remain relevant and competitive?
3. What are the potential barriers to redefining my niche, and how can I overcome them to effectively adapt to new market dynamics?
4. How often should I revisit and reassess my niche to ensure it aligns with my long-term goals and the evolving landscape of my industry?
5. What are successful examples within my field where a business has effectively redefined its niche, and what lessons can I learn from their experience to apply to my own strategic planning?

By contemplating these questions, you can embark on a deliberate path to redefine your niche, ensuring that your business or professional focus is not only aligned with current trends but also positioned for future growth and success.

Global Amplifier 6. Imagine If You Were To Start Again

"The secret of change is to focus all of your energy not on fighting the old, but on building the new." – Socrates

Imagining if you were to start again is a powerful thought experiment that encourages you to break free from the shackles of past decisions and current realities, allowing for a mental and strategic reset. This exercise is not just about wishful thinking; it's a serious strategy tool that can help uncover new paths, rethink approaches, and adapt to the changing landscape of your industry with a fresh perspective. By envisioning a clean slate, armed with the knowledge, resources, and conditions of today, you can identify innovative solutions and strategies that might have been previously overlooked.

Reimagining your professional path involves several steps, starting with a hypothetical restart. Imagine dismantling existing structures and constraints to rebuild your career or business from the ground up. This thought process should incorporate the latest technological advancements, evolving consumer behaviours, and current market dynamics. It's about asking yourself, "What would I do differently with what I know now and the resources available today?"

Reflecting on past experiences is the next critical step. This reflection isn't about dwelling on what went wrong but about learning from both the victories and the challenges.

Reid Hoffman's pathway to co-founding LinkedIn is a masterclass in leveraging past experiences to forge groundbreaking innovations. Before LinkedIn, Hoffman was involved in various ventures, including SocialNet, a social networking service that, while ahead of its time, didn't achieve the success he had hoped for. These early ventures provided Hoffman with invaluable lessons, particularly about the importance of professional networks and the potential of the internet to facilitate connections and opportunities. When he set out to create LinkedIn, Hoffman applied these insights, focusing on creating a platform that could serve as a digital representation of professional relationships and career paths. This vision was based on understanding the limitations of traditional networking and the evolving needs of the professional world in the digital age. LinkedIn's strategy to make professional identities and networks visible online was revolutionary, turning it into an essential tool for professionals worldwide and redefining how career connections are made.

Satya Nadella's tenure at Microsoft illustrates the transformative potential of adopting a startup mindset within a global tech giant. When Nadella took over as CEO in 2014, Microsoft was perceived as lagging behind its competitors, particularly in areas like mobile computing. Nadella's first steps involved a significant cultural shift within the company, encouraging a growth mindset among employees and a focus on innovation, collaboration, and customer-centric products. By 'starting again' and pivoting towards cloud computing and artificial intelligence, Nadella identified and capitalised on emerging technologies that were reshaping the tech landscape. This strategic realignment not only rejuvenated Microsoft's product offerings, such as Azure for cloud services and investments in AI but also repositioned the company as a leader in these domains. Nadella's ability to envision Microsoft with the agility and innovation of a startup catalysed its resurgence, leading to remarkable growth in its valuation and influence in the technology sector.

Both Reid Hoffman and Satya Nadella demonstrate the profound impact of reimagining and reinventing one's approach based on lessons from the past and the possibilities of the present. Their experiences underline the importance of adaptability, strategic foresight, and the willingness to embrace change in pursuit of innovation and success.

These examples demonstrate the transformative potential of starting anew, with a focus on innovation, adaptation, and strategic foresight. They underscore the importance of leveraging your experiences, current market trends, and technological advancements to redefine your approach and trajectory.

Reflective questions to guide this process include:

1. What would I prioritise differently if I were to restart my career or business today, considering the current technological landscape and market conditions?
2. How can the lessons learned from my past successes and failures inform a new beginning, and what changes would they necessitate in my approach?
3. In what ways have emerging technologies and shifts in consumer behaviour created opportunities that I could exploit with a fresh start?
4. How can I apply the 'start-again' mindset to rejuvenate my current projects or business strategies, drawing inspiration from innovative leaders?
5. What steps can I take to systematically reassess and potentially pivot my current trajectory, ensuring it aligns with both my vision and the evolving external environment?

By contemplating these questions, you embark on a mental exercise that not only rejuvenates your strategic thinking but also positions you to navigate the complexities of the modern professional and business landscape with renewed vigour and insight.

End of Section Summary: Personal Ambition and Identity

This section, "Personal Ambition and Identity," lays the foundation for understanding and harnessing the internal forces that drive your success. It challenges you to introspect on your ambitions, asking you to define them on your terms, distinct from the influences and expectations of the external world. Through exploring the essence of your motivation and the identity you forge within your professional landscape, this section sets the stage for genuine growth and achievement.

The journey through this section is about aligning your personal values with your professional aspirations, ensuring that the path you choose resonates deeply with who you are and what you stand for. It encourages a reassessment of who supports your vision and when it might be necessary to pivot your strategy to stay true to your course. This alignment is crucial for setting and achieving goals that not only lead to success but also to personal fulfilment and legacy.

Highlighted by the stories of innovators like Sara Blakely and Richard Branson, this section illustrates the power of self-defined ambition to drive significant change and create lasting impact. Their narratives confirm how a strong sense of personal identity and a clear vision can lead to groundbreaking success, challenging you to consider how your unique strengths and passions can redefine your professional trajectory.

Additionally, this section introduces the 24 Global Amplifiers detailed in this book, accessible and actionable strategies designed to propel you towards achieving your ambitions on a global stage. These amplifiers require nothing more than an internet connection, a curious mind, and the willingness to embrace a broader vision for your life and work. By applying these amplifiers, you embark on a transformative journey, stretching beyond your current boundaries and never returning to your original shape.

Reflective questions at the end of each chapter are prompts and catalysts for deeper exploration and understanding. They invite you to engage with your ambitions and agency actively, challenging you to think bigger, act bolder, and pursue a path of extraordinary, accelerated success.

As you navigate through "Personal Ambition and Identity," you are encouraged to:

- Define ambition on your terms, exploring what truly motivates you and how you can pursue success that aligns with your personal values and passions.
- Assess the support network around you, identifying those who truly champion your vision and considering strategic pivots to align your approach with your evolving ambitions.
- Utilise the 24 Global Amplifiers as tools to explore, experience, and expand your impact on the global stage, leveraging the interconnectedness of our world to amplify your success.

This foundational section prepares you to not only dream bigger but to lay down the actionable steps towards realising those dreams, setting the tone for a journey of growth, innovation, and global influence.

SECTION 'THEM': EXTERNAL INFLUENCES AND MARKET POSITION

In this section, you turn your gaze outward to the ecosystem your business operates within. It challenges you to consider the broader impact of your work and the problems it solves, pushing you to think beyond individual achievements to the legacy you aim to build. This section deals with your place among competitors, colleagues, and collaborators, prompting you to define your unique selling proposition and understand the needs your business fulfils. Through this, 'Them' helps you to navigate the external forces that influence your business and to harness them to fortify your own position in the market.

Global Amplifier 7. Surpass The Limits Set By Others' Achievements

"I am always doing that which I cannot do, in order that I may learn how to do it." – Pablo Picasso

Surpassing the limits set by others' achievements encourages a mindset of continuous growth and innovation, urging individuals to not merely aspire to reach the benchmarks set by predecessors but to extend beyond them. This perspective fosters a culture of excellence and pioneering, where the accomplishments of others serve not as ceilings but as springboards for further exploration and achievement. It emphasises the importance of personal ambition, creativity, and the relentless pursuit of progress.

Understanding that achievements by others are milestones in their unique journeys can inspire us to chart our paths, unbounded by the accomplishments that precede us. It's essential to recognise that while the successes of others can illuminate possibilities, they should not circumscribe our aspirations. Each individual's potential is distinct, with unique contributions to make, unshackled by the precedents of others.

Katherine Johnson's story is a testament to the transformative impact of surpassing the confines of societal and professional expectations. As a mathematician at NASA, Johnson's exceptional skills in celestial navigation were instrumental in the success of the United States' manned spaceflights, including the Apollo 11 moon landing mission. Operating in an era when African American women faced significant discrimination, Johnson's achievements shattered the pervasive racial and gender stereotypes, charting a new course for women and minorities in science and engineering. Her work demonstrated that excellence knows no racial or gender boundaries, inspiring countless individuals to pursue careers in STEM fields previously deemed out of reach. Johnson's legacy is a beacon of perseverance and intelligence, illustrating that breaking through barriers can lead to monumental contributions to humanity's progress.

Chef Massimo Bottura, on the other hand, confirms how challenging the status quo within traditional disciplines can revolutionise perceptions and elevate a field. Bottura's Osteria Francescana, located in Modena, Italy, is more than just a restaurant; it's an emblem of culinary innovation that respects tradition while boldly pushing its boundaries. Through dishes that creatively deconstruct and reimagine Italian classics, Bottura has challenged and expanded the very definition of Italian cuisine. His approach blends art, history, and gastronomy, turning each meal into an explorative experience that transcends conventional dining. This innovative spirit has not only garnered Bottura individual acclaim, including Michelin stars and top rankings in The World's 50 Best Restaurants list, but also propelled the global culinary world into a new era of creativity and exploration. Bottura's journey encourages chefs and creatives alike to explore beyond the familiar, proving that innovation can honour tradition while charting new territories of excellence.

These narratives of Katherine Johnson and Massimo Bottura are powerful reminders of the impact that individuals can have when they dare to exceed the limits set by societal norms, historical precedents, and traditional practices. Their stories underscore the importance of ambition, creativity, and the courage to venture into uncharted territories.

Reflective questions to explore this mindset include:

1. How can I redefine my goals to reflect my highest potential, rather than confining them within the boundaries of what has already been achieved by others?

2. In what ways can I draw inspiration from the achievements of trailblazers like Katherine Johnson and Massimo Bottura to innovate and push boundaries in my field?

3. What specific steps can I take to cultivate a mindset that seeks to surpass rather than merely meet the standards set by others' accomplishments?

4. How can identifying and focusing on a unique problem or niche within my field enable me to go beyond existing achievements and contribute something new?

5. What are the personal or external barriers I need to overcome to not only achieve but exceed the benchmarks set by predecessors in my area of interest?

Engaging with these questions can help individuals to unlock their potential, encouraging them to envision and achieve milestones that extend beyond the accomplishments of others, thereby contributing uniquely to their fields and society at large.

Global Amplifier 8. Confirm The Problem That You Solve And Where It Exists In The World

"Problems are not stop signs, they are guidelines." – Robert H. Schuller

Understanding the problem you solve and its global presence is fundamental to crafting solutions that are both impactful and relevant across diverse contexts. This inquiry not only demands a deep dive into the nature of the challenge your skills, product, or service are aimed at addressing but also necessitates a broad overview of how this issue manifests globally. The incorporation of big data into this process amplifies your ability to grasp the problem's nuances and scale, offering a more comprehensive picture that transcends local or initial perceptions.

Starting with a clear articulation of the problem is critical. Whether it's bridging a gap in the market, fulfilling unmet customer needs, or offering a novel solution to an old problem, understanding the core issue is the first step. This clarity ensures that your efforts are targeted and effective.

Exploring the global existence of the problem involves recognising its various manifestations across different cultures, economies, and ecosystems. Big data plays a pivotal role here, providing insights into patterns, trends, and the problem's pervasiveness that might not be visible at a surface level. Such a data-driven approach not only validates your initial understanding but also potentially broadens the scope of your solution, making it applicable to a wider audience.

Muhammad Yunus's establishment of Grameen Bank is a landmark case of how innovative thinking can transform a localised issue into a solution with worldwide resonance. Yunus, confronting the stark reality of poverty in Bangladesh, recognized that one of the critical barriers for the poor was the lack of access to credit. Traditional banks were unwilling to lend to those without collateral, effectively excluding vast segments of the population from entrepreneurial activities that could elevate their economic status. Yunus's solution was simple yet revolutionary: provide small, collateral-free loans to the impoverished, particularly women, to empower them to start their businesses. This microfinance model not only facilitated economic development within Bangladesh but also became a blueprint for poverty alleviation globally. It demonstrated that financial services tailored to the needs of the poor could be both sustainable and transformative, challenging the conventional banking model and redefining the approach to economic development.

The use of big data by conservation groups to address environmental challenges is another illustrative example of innovative problem-solving with global implications. These organisations collect and analyse vast amounts of environmental data from around the world, gaining insights into patterns and trends that were previously invisible. This data-driven approach allows them to understand the complex dynamics of issues like deforestation, pollution, and the effects of climate change with unprecedented clarity. Armed with this information, conservation strategies can be designed with a high degree of specificity and effectiveness, targeting the most critical areas and employing the most suitable interventions. For instance, satellite imagery and ground data can reveal deforestation hotspots, enabling targeted reforestation efforts and the protection of endangered habitats. Similarly, air and water quality data can inform pollution control measures tailored to the needs of specific regions. This precision in conservation efforts ensures that resources are utilised efficiently, maximising the impact of environmental protection and sustainability initiatives.

These examples underscore the transformative potential of addressing widespread challenges with innovative and adaptable solutions. Yunus's microfinance model and the data-driven strategies employed by conservation groups highlight the power of creative approaches in solving global problems. They highlight how understanding the intricacies of local issues can lead to the development of solutions with far-reaching benefits, advancing economic development and environmental sustainability on a global scale.

Reflective questions to guide this exploration include:

1. How can I more effectively utilise big data to uncover the global dimensions and nuances of the problem I am addressing?
2. What steps can I take to ensure my solution is adaptable and relevant across different cultural and geographical contexts, as seen in the success of Grameen Bank's microfinance model?
3. How can the use of big data inform my understanding of the problem's prevalence and variations worldwide, similar to how conservation groups pinpoint environmental challenges?
4. In what ways can I leverage insights from global data to innovate and enhance the solutions I offer, ensuring they are both impactful and sustainable on a global scale?
5. Considering the global nature of many challenges, how can I collaborate with international partners or leverage cross-border insights to refine and scale my solutions?

By engaging with these questions, you position yourself to craft solutions that not only address the immediate problem but also contribute to global efforts in solving widespread challenges. This comprehensive approach, informed by data and a deep understanding of the issue at hand, paves the way for meaningful, long-lasting impact.

Global Amplifier 9. The World's Unmet Needs Contain Your Biggest Commercial Opportunity

"Find a need and fill it." – Ruth Stafford Peale

The idea that global unmet needs present significant commercial opportunities underscores the potential for innovative solutions to effectively address these challenges. Entrepreneurs and businesses are encouraged to look beyond the broad scope of issues outlined by entities like the United Nations with its Sustainable Development Goals (SDGs), identifying specific niches where they can make a substantial impact. The acknowledgment by UN Secretary-General António Guterres that the SDGs are not fully met highlights a vast field for agile businesses to make a difference.

Global initiatives such as the UN SDGs, Singularity University's Global Grand Challenges, the World Economic Forum's Global Risks Report, and the Bill & Melinda Gates Foundation's Areas of Focus outline the world's pressing needs. These frameworks call for action to end poverty, protect the planet, and ensure prosperity for all, covering areas from education and clean energy to health and sustainable economic growth. They emphasise the role of technology and innovation in solving these issues, presenting entrepreneurs with opportunities to create impactful solutions.

By aligning their strategies with these global objectives, businesses can tap into substantial commercial opportunities. This alignment not only drives profitability but also contributes to advancing global development goals, creating a win-win scenario for businesses and society alike.

A prime example of this approach in action is d.light, a social enterprise that provides affordable and accessible solar energy solutions to off-grid communities, primarily in developing countries. d.light has successfully carved a niche by addressing the need for clean energy, demonstrating how focusing on specific global challenges can lead to the establishment of a sustainable and profitable business model. Through its innovative products and financing options like the pay-as-you-go model, d.light has made clean energy accessible to those who need it most, showcasing the profound societal impact businesses can have by addressing unmet needs.

Peter Diamandis's statement, 'The world's biggest problems are the world's biggest business opportunities,' captures the essence of this perspective. It suggests that addressing global challenges is not just a moral obligation but also a strategic pathway to innovation and profitability. Enterprises that venture into areas such as renewable energy, education technology, and health solutions can achieve significant success by offering innovative products or services that solve pressing issues.

This mindset encourages businesses to see global challenges not as obstacles but as catalysts for growth and innovation. By pursuing solutions to complex problems, companies can drive sustainable development and profitability, positioning themselves at the forefront of meaningful and lasting change. This approach highlights how business can indeed be a powerful force for good in the world, turning the pursuit of global betterment into a journey of commercial success and societal impact.

Reflective questions to explore this concept further include:

1. How can my unique skills or business offering be aligned with the specific, unmet needs outlined in the UN's SDGs, creating a niche market opportunity?
2. What innovative approaches can I adopt to address these challenges effectively, leveraging my entity's agility and capacity for rapid innovation?
3. In which areas of the SDGs do I see the most potential for impactful intervention that aligns with my business's strengths and values?
4. How can I ensure that my solution not only addresses a specific unmet need but also contributes to the overarching goal of sustainable global development?
5. What strategies can I implement to navigate the complexities of global markets, ensuring my solutions are accessible and relevant to the communities most in need?

By contemplating these questions, businesses and entrepreneurs can identify where their capabilities intersect with the world's most pressing needs. This intersection is where significant commercial opportunities lie, offering the chance to drive forward both business success and global progress.

Global Amplifier 10. Know Your Current And Emerging Competition

"If you do not have a competitive advantage, don't compete." - Jack Welch

Understanding your current and emerging competition in today's interconnected global marketplace requires a deep dive into both the immediate threats and those that may loom on the horizon. The digital era has fundamentally altered the competitive landscape, transforming every online business into a global entity. This transformation means that competition is no longer confined to geographical boundaries. A business in one part of the world can easily become a competitor to another thousands of miles away, thanks to the global reach provided by the internet.

The fintech revolution illustrates the transformative impact of digital innovation on traditional industries. Startups like Revolut and Wise (formerly TransferWise) have been at the forefront of this disruption. Initially launched in specific markets, these companies capitalised on the global dissatisfaction with the traditional banking sector's high fees, complex fee structures, and lacklustre customer service. By adopting a digital-first approach, they offered streamlined, user-friendly alternatives that appealed to a tech-savvy generation eager for financial services that matched their online lifestyles.

Revolut, for instance, started by offering currency exchange services without the exorbitant fees typically charged by banks, and it quickly expanded its portfolio to include banking services like budgeting tools, overseas medical insurance, and cryptocurrency exchange. Wise, on the other hand, made its name by creating a more affordable and transparent way to send money abroad, using the real exchange rate and displaying fees upfront. Their platforms cater to a global audience, enabling customers to manage their finances in multiple currencies with ease. The success of these fintech firms lies not only in their innovative services but also in their ability to scale rapidly, leveraging technology to offer global services from day one. This global reach has put them in direct competition with traditional banks across the world, challenging established financial institutions to innovate or risk obsolescence.

In the retail sector, the dynamic is similarly influenced by the rise of e-commerce giants such as Amazon and Alibaba. These platforms have reshaped the retail landscape, offering consumers unprecedented access to a wide range of products at competitive prices. Their logistical prowess and technological infrastructure allow them to enter new markets with ease, presenting a significant challenge to both local and international retailers. However, these platforms also serve as a double-edged sword. While they pose a competitive threat, they simultaneously offer small and medium-sized enterprises (SMEs) the opportunity to reach a global audience without the need for significant investment in their own logistical and marketing capabilities. SMEs can leverage these platforms to sell their products worldwide, tapping into markets previously beyond their reach.

This duality underscores a key aspect of the digital age: competition and opportunity are two sides of the same coin. For traditional banks and retail businesses, the rise of fintech startups and e-commerce giants necessitates a reevaluation of their business models and customer engagement strategies. To remain competitive, these established entities must embrace digital transformation, focusing on customer experience, and exploring new technologies such as blockchain and artificial intelligence to enhance their service offerings.

Moreover, the case of fintech startups and e-commerce platforms illustrates the importance of agility and customer-centricity in today's business environment. These companies have succeeded by addressing unmet customer needs and by offering more transparent, efficient, and user-friendly services. Their ability to adapt quickly to changing consumer preferences and technological advancements serves as a blueprint for businesses across industries aiming to thrive in the digital age.

To navigate this complex environment, businesses must engage in continuous monitoring of their competitive landscape, including sectors or regions they may not currently consider relevant. For instance, a tech startup focusing on renewable energy solutions might find unexpected competition from automotive companies venturing into electric vehicles and battery storage technologies as part of their diversification strategies.

Reflective questions to consider in this context might include:

1. How does my digital footprint expose me to competition from unexpected sectors or regions, and how can I differentiate my offerings?
2. What tools and strategies can I employ to monitor global trends and identify potential competitors early?
3. How can I assess the threat of new entrants into my market, especially those leveraging disruptive technologies or business models?
4. In what ways can partnerships or collaborations provide a competitive edge against both current and future competitors?
5. How can I leverage customer feedback and market research to anticipate shifts in consumer preferences that might attract new competitors?

By pondering these questions and embedding a culture of agility and continuous innovation, businesses can not only anticipate and respond to current and emerging competition but can also seize opportunities to strengthen their market position in a rapidly evolving global economy.

Global Amplifier 11. Tap Into 5.55 Billion Active Internet Users

"The Internet is becoming the town square for the global village of tomorrow." – Bill Gates

Tapping into the 5.55 billion active internet users worldwide is not merely about reaching a vast audience but engaging with them in meaningful ways through the digital ecosystem. In today's interconnected era, digital platforms offer unprecedented opportunities for growth, influence, and understanding of global consumer trends. The digital economy encompasses a significant portion of the world's total economic activity, making digital platforms essential for leveraging connectivity for business success and social impact.

Ignoring the expansive digital audience can result in missed opportunities for growth and influence, as well as a lack of insight into global consumer trends. A strong digital presence is increasingly becoming a marker of relevance and success in the modern world. Digital platforms such as YouTube and TikTok transcend their roles as entertainment sources to become powerful channels for content dissemination and engagement with a global audience. They enable the sharing of messages and content that can cross cultural and regional barriers, enhancing the scope of influence and engagement.

YouTube personality MrBeast, also known as Jimmy Donaldson, has revolutionised content creation through his unique blend of entertainment, philanthropy, and large-scale challenges. He began his YouTube career focusing on video game-related content but gained massive popularity for his extravagant challenges and philanthropic videos. MrBeast's approach involves giving away large sums of money, cars, houses, or even creating large-scale competitions with significant cash prizes. One of his notable campaigns includes planting 20 million trees through the #TeamTrees initiative, launched in collaboration with the Arbor Day Foundation, demonstrating a remarkable use of digital platforms for environmental activism. By engaging his audience not just for entertainment but for collective action towards social and environmental causes, MrBeast illustrates how digital influencers can mobilise resources and public attention on a grand scale. His success, marked by millions of subscribers and billions of views, earning a top spot on Forbes' Top Creator list in 2023, showcases the power of digital media to foster a community around positive action and substantial global impact.

CrashCourse, on the other hand, leverages digital platforms for educational purposes. Founded by John and Hank Green in 2012, CrashCourse is a YouTube channel that offers free, high-quality educational videos on a wide range of subjects, including science, humanities, and social sciences. The channel breaks down complex topics into manageable, engaging lessons that appeal to learners worldwide. By making learning materials accessible to anyone with internet access, CrashCourse addresses the educational disparity and promotes lifelong learning beyond traditional classroom settings. Its success in reaching millions of viewers highlights how digital platforms can democratise education, making knowledge accessible to a global audience. The channel not only supports formal education but also caters to curious minds seeking to expand their knowledge independently, thereby contributing to the global education landscape in a meaningful way.

Both MrBeast and CrashCourse highlight the transformative potential of digital platforms. MrBeast demonstrates how individual creators can leverage their influence for social good and environmental sustainability, engaging a global audience in meaningful causes. CrashCourse illustrates the power of digital media in breaking down barriers to education, providing high-quality learning experiences that are accessible to all. These examples underscore the vast opportunities digital platforms offer for creating positive change, highlighting the role of content creators in shaping a more informed, engaged, and conscious global community.

By engaging with the internet's extensive network of users, individuals and businesses can amplify their messages and initiatives, reaching a diverse and global audience. This strategy is about more than just expanding reach; it involves a deep understanding of the interconnected world we live in and the use of digital tools to make a significant impact across borders.

Reflective questions to consider include:

1. What types of content can I create that will resonate with a diverse, global audience, and how can I leverage the vast reach of digital platforms to share this content effectively?
2. Which innovative strategies can be employed on digital platforms to spread awareness or drive change in areas I am passionate about, making them relevant both locally and globally?
3. How can I utilise analytics and feedback from digital platforms to refine my strategies and ensure my content is engaging and impactful for a global audience?
4. What are the emerging trends on digital platforms, and how can I align my content or initiatives with these trends to maximise reach and engagement?
5. How can collaboration with other digital creators or platforms amplify the impact of my message or initiative, and what are the best practices for establishing such partnerships?

Exploring these questions can help individuals and businesses harness the power of digital platforms to engage with the global internet population in innovative and impactful ways.

Global Amplifier 12. Break The Mould Of Traditional Pathways To Success

"If you want to succeed you should strike out on new paths, rather than travel the worn paths of accepted success." – John D. Rockefeller

Traditional pathways to success often involve a combination of formal education, socio-economic status, and geographic location. Generally, obtaining a degree from a recognised institution is seen as a crucial step towards securing higher-paying and more prestigious jobs. Socio-economic status also plays a significant role, as individuals from wealthier backgrounds often have access to more resources, better education, and influential networks. Additionally, geographic location can greatly influence opportunities available to a person; living in or near major economic centres or cities often provides greater career options and access to cutting-edge industries compared to more remote areas. These traditional routes, while still prevalent, are increasingly complemented by alternative paths in today's diverse global economy.

Deliberately breaking away from traditional paths to success invites a journey of innovation, self-discovery, and potentially groundbreaking achievements. This non-conformist approach champions the idea of leveraging one's unique strengths, experiences, and viewpoints to forge a path that is both distinct and impactful. The stories of individuals and entities like Vishen Lakhiani of Mindvalley and independent documentary filmmakers confirm the transformative potential that lies in choosing an unconventional route.

Vishen Lakhiani's transition from a technology career to founding Mindvalley is a compelling example of how stepping outside conventional paths can lead to groundbreaking innovations that address gaps within society. Mindvalley stands at the intersection of technology, spirituality, and personal development, offering a suite of courses that delve into subjects not typically covered by traditional educational institutions. This platform has become a pioneer in promoting holistic education, focusing on aspects of human development such as mindfulness, biohacking, emotional intelligence, and personal transformation. Lakhiani's approach underscores the importance of a comprehensive education model that nurtures not only the mind but also the heart and spirit. By leveraging technology to make such learning accessible globally, Mindvalley has created a community of learners who are not just seeking knowledge but are on a journey to improve every facet of their lives. Lakhiani's story is a testament to the power of blending personal passion with technological innovation, creating a global impact and redefining what it means to learn and grow.

On the other hand, independent documentary filmmakers utilising platforms like YouTube illustrate the transformative power of digital media in the world of storytelling and information sharing. These creators sidestep traditional barriers to entry in the film industry, such as the need for theatrical distribution or broadcast deals, to share their work directly with a global audience. This direct-to-audience approach allows for a greater diversity of stories to be told, particularly those that may not attract mainstream media's attention due to their niche appeal or challenging subject matter. The democratisation of filmmaking enabled by digital platforms empowers filmmakers to explore and share unique perspectives, shedding light on underrepresented communities, uncovering hidden truths, and sparking important conversations. By providing a space for these diverse narratives, digital platforms like YouTube not only enrich the global cultural landscape but also promote a more inclusive understanding of the world. This shift represents a significant move towards a more equitable media environment, where the power to define which stories are heard is no longer held by a select few but is instead distributed across a wide array of voices from around the globe.

These examples underscore the broader implications of venturing beyond conventional pathways. By doing so, individuals and organisations open themselves up to exploring creative solutions, engaging with global audiences, and ultimately, contributing to societal progress in unique and meaningful ways.

Reflective questions to delve deeper into this exploration include:

1. What unique strengths and experiences do I possess that could lead to innovative solutions within my field, and how can I leverage them to forge a new path to success?
2. How can I utilise technology and digital platforms to challenge traditional norms and reach a broader audience with my ideas or creations?
3. What are the potential risks and rewards of deviating from established career or professional paths, and how can I strategically navigate these to achieve my goals?
4. Who are the trailblazers in my field or related fields who have successfully carved out unique success paths, and what can I learn from their journeys?
5. How can I foster a mindset and culture, whether personally or within my organisation, that embraces innovation, experimentation, and the breaking of traditional moulds to achieve success?

Engaging with these questions encourages a proactive and creative approach to redefining success. It highlights the importance of self-awareness, strategic risk-taking, and the continuous pursuit of growth and learning. By valuing uniqueness and the courage to challenge the status quo, individuals can discover new avenues for achievement that not only fulfil personal aspirations but also contribute to broader societal progress.

End of Section Summary: External Influences and Market Position

In the "Them" section, we've navigated the external landscape that shapes the context in which your business operates. This exploration is crucial for understanding the broader impact of your work, the unique value you offer, and how you position yourself amid competitors and collaborators. By examining the problems your business solves and identifying where these issues exist globally, you're equipped to make more informed strategic decisions that not only advance your position but also contribute meaningfully to the world.

Key takeaways from this section include the importance of surpassing the achievements of others not as an end goal but as a means to drive innovation and set new benchmarks of excellence. Stories of individuals like Katherine Johnson and Massimo Bottura illustrate the profound impact that can be achieved when you aim beyond established limits, challenging you to envision and reach for your highest potential.

Understanding the global scope of the problems you address is essential for tailoring your solutions to meet diverse needs effectively. The use of big data, as demonstrated by initiatives like Grameen Bank and conservation efforts, highlights the power of informed decision-making in creating solutions that resonate on a global scale.

Moreover, recognising the world's unmet needs as your biggest commercial opportunity urges you to align your business strategies with solving pressing global challenges. This approach not only opens up new markets but also positions your business as a leader in innovation and social impact.

Additionally, keeping a pulse on your current and emerging competition, especially in the digital age, is vital for maintaining a competitive edge. The rise of fintech startups and e-commerce giants serves as a reminder of the dynamic nature of competition and the necessity of continuous innovation to remain relevant.

Lastly, tapping into the vast digital audience of 5.55 billion active internet users offers unparalleled opportunities for growth and engagement. Whether through educational content, social impact campaigns, or leveraging digital platforms for storytelling, the digital world is a fertile ground for expanding your influence and connecting with a global audience.

Reflective questions to consolidate your learning from this section might include:

1. How can I better understand and articulate the unique value my business offers in the context of global challenges and needs?
2. In what ways can I leverage big data to gain deeper insights into the problems my business aims to solve, ensuring my solutions are effective and globally relevant?
3. How can I proactively identify and adapt to emerging competition, especially those leveraging digital innovation, to maintain my market position?
4. What strategies can I employ to effectively engage with the global digital audience, maximising the impact and reach of my business?
5. How can I continuously innovate and adapt my business model to not only meet but exceed the evolving expectations of consumers and the market?

By thoughtfully engaging with these areas, you're better positioned to navigate the complexities of the external environment, harness opportunities for innovation, and create a lasting impact through your work. This section empowers you to strategically align your ambitions with actionable insights, setting the stage for success in a competitive and ever-changing global marketplace.

SECTION 'IT': ENABLING TECHNOLOGY

Technology is the great enabler of our time, and in 'It', you explore how it can catapult your ambitious goals forward. This section dives into the potential of digital tools to expand your reach and amplify your impact, both locally and globally. You'll engage with ways to harness technology not just as a utility but as a strategic ally in scaling your operations and fostering global connections. 'It' is about leveraging innovation to push the boundaries of what's possible, ensuring that your business is not just keeping up, but setting the pace.

Global Amplifier 13. Embrace The Ease Of Expanding Your Worldview

"The measure of intelligence is the ability to change." – Albert Einstein

Embracing the ease with which the internet allows us to expand our worldviews is more than a matter of convenience; it's a necessity in the globally interconnected era we inhabit. The internet breaks down barriers, making it possible to access a wealth of cultures, ideas, and knowledge that can profoundly enrich our understanding of the world and its diverse inhabitants. In doing so, it enhances our ability to communicate and collaborate across cultural divides, which is increasingly vital in both personal and professional spheres.

Duolingo, co-founded by Luis von Ahn, stands as a powerful testament to how the internet can revolutionise education and cultural understanding. This platform transcends traditional language learning barriers by offering free, accessible instruction to people all over the globe. Duolingo's unique approach incorporates gamification, making the process of learning a new language not only more interactive and enjoyable but also more effective. Users progress through levels, earn points, and face challenges, all of which contribute to a deeper engagement with the language. Beyond mere vocabulary and grammar, Duolingo introduces learners to cultural nuances and expressions, thereby fostering a deeper appreciation for the cultures associated with each language. This approach not only educates but also unites a diverse community of learners, encouraging global connections and empathy. Through its innovative use of technology, Duolingo highlights how digital platforms can bridge cultural divides and promote a more interconnected and understanding world.

The internet, as a vast repository of knowledge and perspectives, offers myriad opportunities for expanding one's worldview. Educational platforms like Coursera, Khan Academy, and edX provide access to courses across a spectrum of subjects, taught by experts from prestigious institutions worldwide. These platforms make it possible for anyone with an internet connection to learn about anything from quantum physics to art history, breaking down the financial and geographical barriers that traditionally restrict access to high-quality education. Similarly, news sources such as BBC World News and Al Jazeera play a crucial role in presenting global perspectives, offering insights into the social, political, and economic issues affecting different regions. This access to a variety of viewpoints is essential for developing a well-rounded understanding of global dynamics.

Additionally, the internet facilitates cultural exchange in unprecedented ways. Platforms like Couchsurfing and Meetup allow individuals to meet and interact with people from different backgrounds, offering firsthand experiences of other cultures. Online forums and social media platforms provide spaces for discussions and exchanges that can challenge preconceptions and broaden minds. Meanwhile, virtual reality (VR) experiences and online multiplayer games immerse users in settings and narratives far removed from their own, offering a visceral sense of other realities. Digital libraries and online book clubs extend access to literature from around the world, exposing readers to diverse ideas, stories, and historical contexts.

Together, these resources and platforms embody the internet's capacity to educate, enlighten, and connect. They highlight how digital technology can serve as a powerful tool for cultural immersion and intellectual exploration, opening doors to a richer, more nuanced understanding of our world. By tapping into the internet's potential, individuals can embark on journeys of lifelong learning and cultural discovery, contributing to a more informed, empathetic, and united global community.

Reflective questions to consider for further expanding your worldview include:

1. How can engaging with global news platforms and diverse media sources on the internet help me develop a more nuanced understanding of international affairs and perspectives?
2. What role can online educational platforms play in enhancing my cultural literacy, and how can I integrate this learning into my daily life to foster continuous growth?
3. How can participation in online forums and communities dedicated to cultural exchange and global issues increase my empathy and understanding of the world?
4. In what ways can immersive technologies, such as virtual reality, enrich my experience of and appreciation for cultures and perspectives different from my own?
5. How can I leverage the internet to connect with global experts and enthusiasts in fields I am passionate about, thereby deepening my knowledge and expanding my professional network?

By actively seeking out these opportunities for growth and engagement on the internet, individuals can not only enhance their personal and professional lives but also contribute to a more understanding and empathetic global community.

Global Amplifier 14. Built On Local Success For Global Results

"Don't just think, but act locally and globally." – Jack Ma

The ripple effect of local success into global phenomena underscores the power of scalable and adaptable models in today's interconnected environment. Innovations and initiatives that start in a confined geographical or sectoral space can, with strategic planning and vision, inspire and effect change on a worldwide scale. The journey of ideas from local implementation to global adoption is a testament to the potential of innovative thinking to transcend boundaries, whether it's through microfinance, educational reform, social entrepreneurship, or sustainable practices.

The Grameen Bank's microloan programme, initiated by Muhammad Yunus in Bangladesh, stands as a groundbreaking innovation in the field of microfinance, demonstrating the profound impact of local initiatives on the global stage. This programme was designed to provide small loans to the impoverished without requiring collateral, thereby enabling them to embark on entrepreneurial ventures. The success of Grameen Bank has been pivotal in illustrating the power of microfinance to uplift communities by fostering financial independence and entrepreneurship. Its model has been replicated and adapted worldwide, leading to a global microfinance movement that has transformed millions of lives by providing access to financial services. Grameen

Bank's approach has challenged and changed traditional banking paradigms, showing that financial inclusion is both a viable business model and a catalyst for socio-economic development.

The flipped classroom model, popularised by Salman Khan and Khan Academy, represents another example of how innovative ideas in education can transcend borders and influence global teaching methodologies. This model reverses the traditional learning environment by delivering instructional content, often online, outside of the classroom. It moves activities, including those that may have traditionally been considered homework, into the classroom. This approach allows for an interactive and personalised learning experience, where students can engage directly with the material and receive support from teachers in applying knowledge. The flipped classroom has been adopted in various educational settings around the world, significantly enhancing student engagement and learning outcomes. It illustrates how leveraging technology in education can make learning more accessible and effective for students everywhere.

Bill Drayton's work with Ashoka has been instrumental in promoting social entrepreneurship on a global scale. Drayton's vision of a world where everyone is a changemaker has led to the support of social entrepreneurs who address critical social issues with innovative solutions. Ashoka's fellowship program identifies and backs individuals with systemic-change ideas, enabling them to scale their impact. This model has inspired a worldwide movement towards business as a force for good, leading to the establishment of social enterprises across various sectors. These enterprises not only aim to be financially sustainable but also to address societal challenges, ranging from healthcare and education to environmental sustainability. The concept of social entrepreneurship, as propelled by Ashoka, demonstrates the potential of innovative business models to drive social change, showing that profit and purpose can go hand in hand.

These examples collectively underscore the transformative power of local initiatives in shaping global trends. They highlight the importance of innovation, adaptability, and a commitment to addressing societal needs in creating models that can inspire and effect change on a worldwide scale.

Reflective questions to explore the potential of local successes for global influence include:

1. How can I identify and leverage local innovations in my field that have the potential to be scaled up for global impact, particularly in emerging markets or underserved communities?
2. What strategies can be employed to adapt successful local models, such as microfinance or the flipped classroom, to diverse cultural and economic contexts around the world?
3. How can technology be utilised to amplify the reach and effectiveness of local solutions, turning them into tools for global change, especially in fields like education, healthcare, and sustainable development?
4. What partnerships or collaborations could enhance the scalability of local successes, enabling them to address similar challenges on a global scale effectively?
5. How can lessons learned from the global expansion of local initiatives inform future efforts to innovate and implement solutions that have both local relevance and global applicability?

By pondering these questions, individuals and organisations can tap into the transformative potential of local successes, turning them into catalysts for global change. This approach not only maximises the impact of innovative solutions but also fosters a more interconnected and responsive global community, ready to tackle the challenges of the future together.

Global Amplifier 15. Harness Digital Tools To Connect And Collaborate Globally

"I can do things you cannot, you can do things I cannot; together we can do great things." - Mother Teresa

In today's digital age, the ability to harness technology for global connection and collaboration has become a cornerstone of innovation and progress across industries. The evolution of digital tools has not only made it easier to reach across the vast expanse of our world but has also significantly enhanced the efficiency and scope of collaborative efforts in fields ranging from healthcare to software development, business operations, and beyond.

Telemedicine has fundamentally altered the healthcare landscape by leveraging digital tools to provide medical services, effectively shrinking the distances between healthcare providers and patients. This advancement is particularly significant in remote or underserved areas, where access to medical facilities and specialists is limited. Through telemedicine, patients can receive diagnoses, medical advice, and even prescriptions without leaving their homes, greatly enhancing the accessibility and efficiency of healthcare services. This digital transformation has been instrumental in improving patient outcomes by ensuring timely medical intervention and has opened up new avenues for managing chronic conditions, mental health services, and patient education. The ability of telemedicine to transcend geographical barriers embodies the potential of digital tools to create a more inclusive and equitable healthcare system globally.

In the software development sector, platforms like GitHub have revolutionised how developers collaborate, breaking down the barriers that once hindered collective innovation. GitHub serves as a repository hosting service that facilitates version control and collaboration, making it an essential tool for developers working on joint projects across different geographies. This platform has become a cornerstone of the open-source movement, where developers contribute to each other's work, share knowledge, and accelerate technological advancement. The collaborative environment fostered by GitHub encourages a culture of learning and sharing, significantly speeding up the development process and leading to the creation of more robust and innovative software solutions that benefit the wider community.

For businesses, the integration of communication and collaboration platforms such as Zoom, Slack, and Google Workplace has heralded a new era of operational efficiency and flexibility. These tools have enabled organisations to embrace remote work, allowing them to assemble teams of the best talents from around the world and operate in a truly global marketplace. The ability to collaborate in real-time, share documents, and manage projects without physical constraints has not only reduced operational costs but also increased productivity and employee satisfaction. This shift towards digital workplaces has also allowed businesses to serve their international customers more effectively, adapting to different time zones and cultural nuances with unprecedented agility.

Crowdfunding platforms like Kickstarter and Indiegogo have transformed the landscape of funding for entrepreneurs, artists, and innovators. By allowing individuals to present their ideas directly to a global audience, these platforms have facilitated the realisation of projects that may have otherwise gone unnoticed by traditional funding bodies. This direct line to potential supporters empowers creators to gauge interest, validate their concepts, and secure the necessary resources to bring their visions to life. The success stories emerging from these platforms highlight the power of community support and the shifting dynamics in how projects are funded, moving away from gatekeepers and towards a more democratic model of investment.

In the world of digital marketing, tools like Hootsuite, Buffer, and other advanced marketing technologies have become pivotal in crafting and executing effective global engagement strategies. These platforms empower marketers to orchestrate complex, targeted advertising campaigns and content distribution with precision, ensuring that their messages resonate with the intended audiences across different regions and cultures.

Hootsuite and Buffer, for example, are social media management tools that allow businesses to schedule posts, track social media traffic, and engage with audiences across multiple platforms from a single dashboard. This centralised approach to social media management is invaluable for marketers looking to maintain a consistent and timely online presence, which is crucial for building brand awareness and engagement on a global scale.

Moreover, these tools offer in-depth analytics and insights, enabling marketers to understand their audience's behaviours, preferences, and engagement patterns. By analysing this data, businesses can tailor their content and campaigns to better meet the needs and interests of their target demographics, improving the effectiveness of their marketing efforts. This data-driven approach facilitates more personalised and meaningful interactions with audiences, enhancing customer experience and loyalty.

In addition to social media management, digital marketing technologies encompass a wide range of tools and platforms, including email marketing software, SEO tools, content management systems, and advertising platforms. These technologies enable marketers to execute a comprehensive digital strategy that covers all aspects of online marketing, from content creation and optimisation to email campaigns and paid advertising. By leveraging these tools, businesses can enhance their online visibility, drive traffic to their websites, and convert leads into customers more efficiently.

The global reach provided by digital marketing tools means that businesses can now access international markets with relative ease. Targeted advertising features, such as those offered by Google Ads and Facebook Ads, allow marketers to reach specific audiences based on demographics, interests, location, and even behaviours, making it possible to tailor messages to different cultural contexts and consumer needs. This level of granularity in targeting ensures that marketing resources are used more effectively, maximising ROI and impact.

Reflective questions to ponder include:

1. How can telemedicine and other digital health tools be further leveraged to improve healthcare accessibility and outcomes across different regions of the world?
2. What strategies can be employed to enhance collaborative software development using platforms like GitHub, ensuring more inclusive and diverse participation from the global tech community?
3. In what ways can businesses further adapt digital collaboration tools to enhance productivity and innovation among geographically dispersed teams?
4. How can crowdfunding be utilised to support a wider array of projects, ensuring that innovative ideas receive the backing they need regardless of the geographical location of their creators?
5. What new approaches can be taken to optimise the use of digital marketing tools for reaching and engaging with a global audience, particularly in sectors where online presence is crucial for success?

By exploring these questions, individuals and organisations can better understand how to effectively harness digital tools for global collaboration, ensuring that their initiatives and projects have the widest possible impact and contribute to global progress.

Global Amplifier 16. Build Strategic Connections For Global Reach

"No one can whistle a symphony. It takes a whole orchestra to play it." – H.E. Luccock

Establishing a global network is essential in today's interconnected environment. Utilising platforms like X (formerly known as Twitter) or LinkedIn can be particularly valuable for professionals seeking to gain diverse perspectives and uncover new opportunities. Entrepreneurs in the tech industry, for example, leverage these networks to connect with mentors, investors, and peers worldwide, thereby gaining insights that drive innovation and growth.

Building relationships across borders can unveil a treasure trove of opportunities, ideas, and mutual growth. In this context, the emphasis is on quality rather than quantity, with strategic connections being the cornerstone.

Anna Wintour's adept use of her global network stands as a masterclass in strategic networking within the highly competitive and ever-evolving fashion industry. As the Editor-in-Chief of Vogue and Artistic Director for Condé Nast, Wintour has cultivated a vast and varied network that spans designers, celebrities, business leaders, and influencers across the globe. This network has not only afforded her a unique vantage point from which to view and influence the fashion world but has also enabled her to play a decisive role in its ongoing narrative and development.

Wintour's ability to foster and maintain relationships with key figures in various sectors has been instrumental in her capacity to shape fashion trends and the industry at large. By aligning with designers, she has been pivotal in bringing emerging talents to the forefront, often giving them the platform and visibility needed to succeed in a saturated market. This support extends beyond mere recognition, as Wintour often provides critical guidance and exposure through Vogue's influential pages, thereby directly contributing to the trajectory of designers' careers.

Her network also includes a broad spectrum of celebrities and public figures, whose appearances in Vogue can set the tone for fashion trends and public interest. Wintour's strategic use of celebrity endorsements and features has blurred the lines between fashion, culture, and entertainment, making Vogue a cultural touchstone that transcends its original fashion magazine roots.

Moreover, Wintour's connections with business leaders and influencers have facilitated unique collaborations and sponsorships, further solidifying Vogue's position as a leading authority in fashion. These relationships have enabled the magazine to expand its influence into politics and social issues, reflecting Wintour's personal commitment to addressing broader societal concerns through the lens of fashion.

Her influence extends to hosting the Met Gala, an annual fundraising gala for the benefit of the Metropolitan Museum of Art's Costume Institute in New York City. This event, often dubbed as "fashion's biggest night out," showcases the intricate relationship between fashion and celebrity culture, further influenced by Wintour's curated guest list that includes a who's who of the entertainment industry, politics, and high society.

In essence, Anna Wintour's global network confirms the power of strategic connections in driving innovation, setting trends, and fostering growth within the fashion industry. Her ability to navigate and leverage these relationships underscores the importance of a well-established network for achieving significant impact and influence in any field.

Maintaining solely a local network poses significant risks in our globally connected world. A local-only focus may limit exposure to diverse perspectives, innovative ideas, investments, influence, and new market opportunities, potentially leading to stagnation. It restricts access to a broader talent pool, international partnerships, and insights into global trends, which are vital for staying competitive and relevant.

Moreover, businesses and professionals with exclusively local networks might struggle to adapt to global shifts in their industries, missing out on opportunities for growth and the capacity to scale their operations or influence effectively.

By focusing on building and nurturing strategic connections, one can establish a foundation for global reach, leveraging the collective knowledge, resources, and opportunities that a diverse professional network offers.

Reflective Questions:

1. How can professionals actively develop and engage with a global professional network, ensuring it encompasses a variety of countries and cultures?
2. What strategies can be implemented to foster significant connections within this global community, potentially leading to collaborative or commercial outcomes in my field?
3. In what ways can individuals overcome cultural and linguistic barriers to build effective and meaningful global networks?
4. How can technology and social media platforms be optimised to enhance global networking efforts, particularly in industries less represented on traditional platforms?
5. What role does mentorship play in expanding a global network, and how can one both find and become a mentor in an international context?

By contemplating these questions, individuals can better strategise their approach to global networking, ensuring they build a diverse, influential, and strategically advantageous professional network.

Global Amplifier 17. Leverage Insight And Learning With AI

"Artificial Intelligence has the potential not just to revolutionise the future, but to completely transform the way we think about the present." – Nick Bostrom

Expanding upon the importance of leveraging Artificial Intelligence (AI) for insights and learning reveals the transformative impact AI technologies can have across diverse sectors. The capability of AI to process and analyse copious amounts of data offers unparalleled opportunities for deepening understanding and fostering innovation. Neglecting to utilise AI for these purposes can result in missed opportunities for leveraging advanced analytics, making less informed decisions, and failing to keep pace with the rapid technological advancements and data-driven insights that are redefining industries.

The integration of (AI) in various fields marks a transformative shift towards more data-driven and informed decision-making processes. Its application ranges from environmental science to business intelligence and customer engagement, showcasing AI's versatility and impact.

Environmental Science and Sustainability:

AI algorithms are instrumental in parsing through and analysing extensive climate data, offering predictions and insights that are crucial for crafting sustainability strategies. This facet of AI is pivotal in combating climate change, as it aids in modelling complex environmental scenarios and informs policy-making. Companies like IBM are at the forefront of this movement, using AI to enhance weather forecasting, improve energy efficiency, and develop sustainable practices. AI's predictive capabilities enable these companies to anticipate environmental trends and respond proactively, thus playing a key role in efforts to mitigate climate change and its effects.

Business Intelligence and Consumer Insights:

In business, AI's ability to analyse social media and digital platform data has become invaluable. Companies like Brandwatch employ AI to monitor consumer sentiment and trends, providing businesses with essential insights into public opinion. This information is critical for companies aiming to tailor their marketing strategies, product development, and customer engagement to better align with consumer needs and societal shifts. Through real-time data analysis, AI enables businesses to stay ahead of market trends and maintain a competitive edge.

Education and Customer Service:

AI chatbots, such as ChatGPT, represent a significant advancement in how individuals access information. These AI tools, with their conversational interface, have made learning more accessible and personalised to individual preferences. This revolution extends beyond personal use to businesses and educational institutions, which utilise chatbots to enhance customer service, provide educational support, and engage audiences more effectively. By offering a direct and interactive means of communication, AI chatbots bridge the gap between businesses or educational providers and their audiences, facilitating a more engaged and informed public.

Strategic Integration of AI:

Integrating AI into strategies for insight and learning enables organisations to remain at the forefront of technological advancements, utilising the power of data-driven insights to inform decisions and foster innovation in their respective fields. The risk of overlooking AI's potential is significant; it can result in falling behind in an increasingly data-oriented world. Therefore, beginning to experiment with AI technologies, such as ChatGPT, is advised as an entry point into the broader AI landscape. While premium versions of AI tools may offer enhanced capabilities, the key is to start engaging with AI technology to understand its potential and application in your field.

Reflective Questions:

1. How can AI be leveraged to predict and address future challenges in my field, especially those related to sustainability and environmental impact?
2. In what ways can AI-driven insights into consumer behaviour and trends inform my business strategies, and how can I ensure these strategies remain ethically grounded and consumer-focused?
3. How can AI chatbots and conversational interfaces be optimised to improve learning experiences and customer engagement within my organisation? What metrics can I use to measure success?
4. Considering the vast amount of data available, how can I ensure the AI systems I implement are interpreting this data accurately and providing insights that are truly beneficial for decision-making?
5. As AI continues to evolve, what steps can I take to stay informed about the latest developments and potential applications in my industry? How can I foster a culture of innovation and openness to new technologies within my team or organisation?

These questions encourage a thoughtful examination of how AI can be integrated into various aspects of professional practice, from enhancing sustainability efforts to refining customer engagement strategies. Engaging with these questions can help individuals and organisations to more effectively harness the power of AI for insight, innovation, and impact.

Global Amplifier 18. Design For One World, Diminishing Borders And Barriers

"The Earth is what we all have in common." - Wendell Berry

Designing for one world, diminishing borders and barriers, represents a forward-thinking approach that acknowledges the interconnectedness of our global community. This philosophy encourages the removal of traditional constraints in thinking and operations, advocating for solutions that serve a broader, more diverse audience. As the digital age accelerates the blurring of geographical and cultural lines, adopting a global perspective becomes not just beneficial but imperative for those seeking to innovate and make a meaningful impact across industries.

The "Overview Effect," a term coined by space philosopher Frank White, captures a profound shift in awareness reported by astronauts during spaceflight, when they first view the Earth from space. This cognitive shift brings about a deep understanding of Earth's fragility and the artificial nature of political borders, fostering a sense of global solidarity and shared destiny among humanity. Astronaut Edgar Mitchell's experiences emphasise the interconnectedness of all life and the importance of adopting a holistic, planetary perspective in tackling global issues. This perspective is increasingly pertinent in a world where digital connectivity and global challenges demand solutions that transcend national and cultural divisions. The Overview

Effect symbolises the imperative to embrace a global viewpoint, urging innovators and leaders to consider the broader impact of their actions on the global community and to strive for solutions that promote planetary well-being.

The transformation brought about by remote work and digital nomadism is a testament to the diminishing relevance of physical and geographical barriers in the modern workplace. The widespread adoption of digital communication tools has ushered in a new era of work, where flexibility, autonomy, and global connectivity redefine what it means to be part of a workforce. This shift not only democratises access to opportunities but also encourages a more inclusive and diverse professional environment. Businesses that embrace this trend can harness a wealth of global talent, fostering innovation and cultural exchange, and ultimately achieving a competitive edge in the global marketplace.

IKEA's approach to design and retail highlights how a company can successfully navigate the complexities of global commerce by marrying universal design principles with a sensitivity to local tastes and regulations. By maintaining a core ethos of affordability, functionality, and aesthetic appeal, IKEA's products resonate with consumers worldwide, while localised adaptations ensure alignment with specific cultural preferences and legal requirements. This balance between global appeal and local relevance has cemented IKEA's position as a leader in the global home furnishings market, demonstrating the commercial and cultural benefits of a globally minded business strategy.

Doctors Without Borders (Médecins Sans Frontières) embodies the spirit of global humanitarianism, operating on the conviction that access to medical care is a universal right that supersedes political and cultural barriers. By mobilising medical professionals to provide care in crisis zones, natural disasters, and epidemics, the organisation demonstrates how commitment to a global cause can unite diverse groups in the pursuit of a common goal. Their work not only alleviates suffering in the immediate term but also sets a precedent for international cooperation and solidarity, challenging the world to view health care as a global responsibility rather than a matter of national policy or capability.

These examples collectively illustrate the power and necessity of adopting a global perspective in today's interconnected world. Whether in business, humanitarian efforts, or the evolution of work culture, the ability to see beyond immediate contexts and consider the global implications of actions is crucial for addressing the complex challenges of the 21st century.

Reflective questions to consider in adopting a borderless design philosophy include:

1. How can I incorporate a global perspective into my projects or solutions, ensuring they address the needs of diverse populations across different cultures and regions?
2. What strategies can I employ to leverage digital technologies for broader reach and impact, mirroring the flexibility and inclusivity of the remote work trend?
3. In what ways can the principles of the "Overview Effect" inform my approach to problem-solving and innovation, fostering a sense of global unity and cooperation?
4. How can I balance the need for universal appeal with the necessity of localising my offerings to meet specific cultural or regulatory requirements, similar to IKEA's approach?
5. What lessons can be learned from the operations of Doctors Without Borders in designing services that are not only globally relevant but also adaptable to local needs and challenges?

By exploring these questions, individuals and organisations can begin to navigate the complexities of a borderless world, designing solutions that are not only innovative and globally relevant but also contribute to a more connected and inclusive global community.

End of Section Summary: Enabling Technology

The "It" section underscores the transformative role of technology in expanding the scope and impact of businesses on a global scale. It delves into a number of ways digital tools and platforms can be harnessed to not only enhance operational efficiency but also to foster connections that transcend geographical boundaries. This exploration highlights the necessity of integrating technology as a strategic component of business planning, with a focus on leveraging innovation to navigate the challenges and opportunities presented by our rapidly evolving digital landscape.

Key insights from this section include:

Global Perspective Through Technology: The ease of accessing diverse cultures and ideas via the internet, as illustrated by Duolingo's approach to language learning, emphasises technology's role in broadening our worldviews. This expanded perspective is crucial for businesses aiming to operate on a global scale, ensuring they remain sensitive to cultural nuances and informed about international trends.

Local Innovations with Global Impact: The journey from local success to global influence, demonstrated by the microfinance model of Grameen Bank and the flipped classroom concept, showcases the potential of scalable solutions to address widespread challenges. These examples highlight the importance of thinking locally while acting globally, using technology to adapt and extend the reach of innovative ideas.

Collaboration Across Borders: The digital era has redefined collaboration, enabling teams to work together seamlessly regardless of physical location. This shift towards a more interconnected workforce is underpinned by the widespread adoption of platforms like Zoom and Slack, which facilitate communication and project management across global teams, thereby enhancing productivity and innovation.

Strategic Global Networking: Building and nurturing a global professional network, as demonstrated by the strategic connections of industry leaders like Anna Wintour, underscores the importance of leveraging digital platforms for networking. These connections can open doors to new opportunities, insights, and collaborations, driving personal and professional growth on an international scale.

Leveraging AI for Global Insights: The potential of AI to provide deep insights and facilitate learning across various sectors highlights the critical role of technology in driving forward-looking strategies. Whether it's in environmental science, business intelligence, or education, AI's ability to process vast amounts of data can inform more effective decision-making and innovative solutions.

Designing for One World: The concept of designing solutions that diminish borders and barriers is more relevant than ever in our interconnected world. This approach, inspired by insights such as the Overview Effect experienced by astronauts, encourages a holistic view of our global community, advocating for solutions that are inclusive, sustainable, and universally accessible.

Reflective questions to further integrate the insights from this section include:

1. How can I further leverage technology to enhance my business's global reach and operational efficiency?
2. In what ways can I contribute to global solutions through local innovations, using technology to scale these ideas effectively?

3. How can I optimise digital tools and platforms to foster collaboration and innovation within my global network?
4. What strategies can I employ to ensure my business remains adaptable and responsive to the rapid technological changes shaping our world?

By engaging with these themes, businesses and individuals can navigate the complexities of the digital age with greater agility and vision. The "It" section serves as a reminder of the pivotal role of technology in enabling businesses to achieve unprecedented levels of connectivity, efficiency, and global impact, setting the stage for a future where technology-driven solutions lead the way in solving the world's most pressing challenges.

SECTION 'TOGETHER': COLLECTIVE SUCCESS AND COMMUNITY

Success is rarely a solo endeavour, and 'Together' underscores the power of collective ambition and strategic alliances. This section delves into the dynamics of working with established powers and creating new partnerships that can redefine market norms. It asks how collaboration and community can act as force multipliers for your vision, and how by working together, breakthroughs that once seemed like moonshots become attainable. 'Together' is about finding strength in numbers and making the leap from individual success to collective triumph.

Global Amplifier 19. Aim For The Moon To Maximise Breakthroughs

"We choose to go to the moon in this decade and do the other things, not because they are easy, but because they are hard." – John F. Kennedy

Aiming for the moon to maximise breakthroughs is not just an aspirational phrase but a strategic approach that encourages pushing the limits of what's considered achievable. This mindset, inspired by the monumental success of the Apollo 11 mission, serves as a metaphor for setting highly ambitious goals that challenge the status quo and propel individuals and organisations towards innovation and remarkable accomplishments. The essence of a "moonshot" lies in its capacity to drive significant advancements by aiming beyond current limitations, fostering a culture where daring to dream big is the norm rather than the exception.

The importance of setting audacious goals transcends mere ambition; it is a critical element in catalysing change and achieving substantial progress. While a conservative approach might ensure steady progress, it seldom leads to the kind of transformative change or disruptive innovation necessary to solve complex problems or redefine industries.

The narratives of Fauja Singh and Erin Brockovich illustrate the profound impact of setting and pursuing audacious goals, demonstrating how individuals can transcend conventional boundaries and effect significant change.

Fauja Singh, known affectionately as the "Turbaned Tornado," embarked on marathon running in his eighties, a feat that defies common perceptions about ageing and physical capability. At an age when most would consider physical exertion a risk, Singh took to one of the most challenging forms of it, marathon running, proving not just his physical endurance but also the limitless potential of the human spirit. His journey to becoming the oldest person to complete a full marathon is a powerful testament to the idea that age is but a number, and true determination knows no age limit. Singh's achievements have inspired people around the world to reassess and often discard their own self-imposed limitations, encouraging a broader societal shift towards a more inclusive understanding of physical fitness and capability in advanced age.

Erin Brockovich's story is another remarkable example of surpassing perceived limitations, this time in the field of legal advocacy and environmental activism. Without a formal legal education, Brockovich played a pivotal role in building a case against the Pacific Gas and Electric Company of California in 1993 for contaminating the drinking water of Hinkley, California, with hexavalent chromium. Her unwavering dedication, meticulous research, and ability to rally affected communities led to a historic settlement of $333 million in 1996, the largest of its kind in U.S. history at the time. Brockovich's work went beyond winning a lawsuit; it underscored the power of grassroots advocacy and the impact an individual can have on public health and corporate accountability. Her story has become a beacon of hope for many, demonstrating that with tenacity and passion, individuals can take on seemingly insurmountable challenges and emerge victorious.

These stories are not just tales of personal triumph but are emblematic of a broader principle: the extraordinary is within reach for those who dare to aim beyond the conventional. Singh and Brockovich, through their actions, challenge us to reconsider what we perceive as limits and to redefine the boundaries of our potential.

Innovation, at its core, requires a willingness to take risks and embrace challenges that seem insurmountable. A moonshot mindset fosters an environment where creative problem-solving thrives, and breakthrough innovations can emerge. It encourages looking beyond immediate obstacles and envisioning a future where bold ideas have transformed reality. This approach is vital in today's fast-paced, technology-driven world, where the next big breakthrough could be just an ambitious goal away.

Reflective questions to guide the pursuit of your moonshot include:

1. What groundbreaking goal within my field or interest could redefine existing standards and how might I pursue it?
2. How can I foster a culture, either within my organisation or personal life, that encourages taking calculated risks towards achieving high-impact goals?
3. What lessons can I learn from individuals like Fauja Singh and Erin Brockovich about perseverance and dedication in the face of daunting challenges?
4. In planning for a moonshot, what steps can I take to balance ambition with strategic planning and realistic assessment of resources and timelines?
5. How can I leverage collaboration and seek out innovative partnerships to enhance the feasibility and impact of my moonshot goal?

By contemplating these questions, individuals and organisations can chart a course towards not just incremental improvements but towards groundbreaking achievements that have the potential to leave a lasting legacy.

Global Amplifier 20. Question The Value Established Powers And Intermediaries

"You never change things by fighting the existing reality. To change something, build a new model that makes the existing model obsolete." – Buckminster Fuller

Challenging established powers and intermediaries is a critical step towards fostering innovation, achieving greater independence, and potentially transforming entire industries. This approach involves questioning the necessity and efficiency of traditional systems and structures that have long dominated various fields. By doing so, individuals and organisations can unlock new opportunities for creativity, direct engagement with audiences or markets, and the development of more sustainable and ethical practices.

Stella McCartney's foray into sustainable and cruelty-free fashion represents a pivotal shift in the fashion industry, challenging long-standing practices and setting new standards for environmental and ethical responsibility. McCartney's brand is built on a foundation of sustainability, eschewing animal products and prioritising eco-friendly materials and production methods. This commitment has not only distinguished her label in a competitive industry but also catalysed a significant change in consumer behaviour and industry norms. By proving that luxury and fashion can coexist with sustainability, McCartney has inspired both emerging and established designers to reconsider their materials and methods, contributing to a gradual but perceptible shift towards more responsible fashion practices. Her influence extends beyond the runway, encouraging consumers to demand transparency and ethical considerations from the brands they support, thereby fostering a culture of accountability within the industry.

Amanda Hocking's journey from unknown writer to self-publishing sensation underscores the transformative power of digital technology in the publishing world. Hocking, who turned to self-publishing after numerous rejections from traditional publishers, utilised platforms like Amazon to sell her novels directly to readers. Her success story - selling millions of copies and securing a significant profit - demonstrated that authors no longer need to rely on the conventional publishing model to achieve recognition and financial success. Hocking's achievements have empowered a new generation of writers to explore self-publishing as a viable and potentially lucrative path, significantly democratising the process of publishing. This shift has prompted traditional publishing houses to reassess their roles and offerings in a rapidly evolving market, where direct engagement between authors and readers can flourish without intermediaries.

These examples underscore the potential impact of challenging conventional pathways and the power of leveraging technology and innovation to redefine success. They highlight the importance of autonomy in creation and distribution processes and the significant benefits of establishing a more direct relationship with consumers.

Reflective questions to explore when considering challenging established powers and intermediaries include:

1. How can I identify outdated or inefficient practices within my industry, and what innovative approaches can I adopt to address or circumvent these issues?
2. What role do established powers and intermediaries currently play in my field, and are there more direct, efficient, or ethical alternatives available to achieve similar or better outcomes?

3. Inspired by the examples of Stella McCartney and Amanda Hocking, what unique values or perspectives do I bring to my work that could lead to industry-wide change or innovation?

4. How can I leverage technology and digital platforms to bypass traditional intermediaries and establish a more direct connection with my audience or market?

5. In what ways can challenging the status quo in my professional endeavours not only benefit my career but also contribute to broader societal or environmental progress?

Addressing these questions can inspire a strategic reevaluation of how to operate within and potentially disrupt traditional industry models. It encourages a proactive stance towards innovation, emphasising the importance of direct engagement and the pursuit of practices that align with modern values and technological advancements.

Global Amplifier 21. Aim Big To Unlock Potential (10X Versus 10%)

"The ones who are crazy enough to think that they can change the world, are the ones who do." – Steve Jobs

Aiming big to unlock potential, epitomised by the concept of '10X thinking' as opposed to the more traditional approach of aiming for a mere 10% improvement, fundamentally shifts the focus from mere incremental progress to striving for radical, transformative change. This bold approach to goal-setting and problem-solving is predicated on the belief that by setting vastly ambitious goals, individuals and organisations can catalyse innovation and achieve breakthroughs that redefine what's possible.

Astro Teller, the captain of Moonshots at X (formerly Google X), champions the philosophy of '10X thinking,' a mindset that urges the pursuit of solutions that are ten times better, not just ten percent improvements. This ambitious approach is predicated on the belief that aiming for exponential rather than incremental advancements can lead to breakthrough innovations. Teller and his team at X undertake "moonshot" projects - endeavours that address massive challenges through radical solutions and the application of breakthrough technologies. This methodology is based on the understanding that while aiming high might increase the risk of failure, it also opens the door to transformative success that can fundamentally alter how we live and interact with the world.

James Dyson's relentless experimentation and refusal to accept the limitations of traditional vacuum technology led to the development of the world's first bagless vacuum cleaner using cyclonic separation. This innovation dramatically improved efficiency and performance, setting a new industry standard and establishing Dyson as a leading brand in home appliances. Dyson's journey underscores the essence of '10X thinking'—the conviction that significant problems require bold solutions, not just minor adjustments.

Similarly, the Wright Brothers, Orville and Wilbur, did not content themselves with making incremental improvements to existing glider designs. Instead, they embarked on a quest to achieve powered, controlled flight, a goal that seemed nearly insurmountable at the time. Their success in 1903 with the first successful powered flights in Kitty Hawk, North Carolina, did more than just improve aviation; it launched humanity into the aerial age, reshaping the future of travel and marking the dawn of a new era in human mobility.

The ethos of '10X thinking' embodies the spirit of exploration and innovation. It challenges individuals and organisations to think beyond the confines of current capabilities and to envision what could be accomplished if the fear of failure was set aside in favour of bold, transformative ambitions. This approach not only drives technological and scientific advancements but also encourages a culture of creativity and relentless pursuit of improvement.

Reflective questions to encourage '10X thinking' include:

1. What long-standing challenges in my field could benefit from a '10X thinking' approach, and how can I begin to conceptualise solutions that are not just better, but revolutionary?
2. How can I cultivate a mindset that consistently seeks transformative change over incremental improvements, especially in areas where progress has plateaued?

3. What are the potential barriers to adopting a '10X thinking' approach in my current projects or goals, and how can I strategise to overcome them?

4. Considering the examples of James Dyson and the Wright Brothers, what lessons can I apply from their experiences to my pursuit of groundbreaking innovation?

5. How can I leverage collaboration and diverse perspectives to fuel '10X thinking' in my team or organisation, encouraging bold ideas and challenging the status quo?

By pondering these questions, individuals and organisations can unlock new dimensions of creativity and innovation, pushing beyond traditional boundaries to explore uncharted territories of growth and development.

Global Amplifier 22. Confirm Your Dedicated Audience To Co-Design With (1000 True Fans)

"Alone we can do so little; together we can do so much." – Helen Keller

Kevin Kelly's theory of 1,000 true fans has significantly altered the landscape for artists, creators, and entrepreneurs by proposing an alternative pathway to success that diverges from the traditional reliance on mass appeal. This theory suggests that achieving sustainable success does not necessitate broad, mainstream recognition but can instead be attained through the cultivation of a dedicated following. According to Kelly, if creators can garner a core group of 1,000 fans who are willing to spend a certain amount each year to support their work, they can achieve a sustainable living. This concept emphasises the power of quality over quantity in building an audience or customer base.

The essence of the 1,000 true fans model lies in its focus on fostering deep, meaningful connections with a relatively small group of people who are highly engaged and committed to the creator's work. These true fans are distinguished by their willingness to go beyond passive consumption; they actively support the creator through financial contributions, word-of-mouth promotion, and by participating in a community centred around the creator's work. This level of engagement ensures a stable and predictable income stream for the creator, providing the freedom to focus on their craft without the pressure to cater to the lowest common denominator for the sake of broader appeal.

Moreover, the theory challenges the conventional metrics of success that equate popularity with success, offering a more nuanced and attainable definition of achievement. It acknowledges the value of niche markets and the potential for creators to thrive within them, leveraging the direct-to-consumer models facilitated by digital platforms. This approach not only enables creators to maintain creative control and authenticity but also fosters a closer, more personal relationship with their audience, enhancing the overall quality of the engagement.

In the context of today's digital landscape, the feasibility of connecting with a specific, dedicated audience has dramatically increased. Direct-to-consumer platforms like Patreon have revolutionised the creator-audience relationship by providing the tools necessary to build these deep connections. Creators can offer exclusive content, behind-the-scenes access, and personalised experiences that are not available to the general public. This not only incentivizes fan support but also fosters a sense of community and belonging among the audience, strengthening their emotional investment in the creator's success.

Sarah Andersen's strategic use of Patreon confirms the transformative potential of direct-to-consumer platforms in enabling creators to sustain their careers through the support of a dedicated fanbase. Andersen, known for her webcomic "Sarah's Scribbles," has adeptly harnessed Patreon to bridge the gap between her and her audience, creating a reciprocal relationship that benefits both parties. By providing her fans with unique content and experiences that are not accessible elsewhere, Andersen offers tangible value to her supporters, incentivising their financial contributions and fostering a sense of exclusivity and community.

This approach has several key advantages. First, it allows Andersen to directly monetize her fanbase without relying on traditional advertising or publishing models, which often take a significant cut of the creators' earnings. Second, the platform facilitates a closer relationship with her audience, enabling Andersen to receive immediate feedback on her work. This feedback loop is invaluable for creative evolution, as it provides insights into what resonates with her audience, guiding future projects and content.

Moreover, Andersen's Patreon community acts as a collaborative partner in the creative process. Fans who are deeply invested in Andersen's work often provide not just feedback but also ideas and inspiration, contributing to a co-creative environment that enriches Andersen's content. This participatory model blurs the line between creator and consumer, leading to a more engaged and loyal fanbase.

The financial viability afforded by this model cannot be overstated. With a steady stream of income from her true fans, Andersen can focus on creating content that she and her audience care about, rather than content designed to appeal to the broadest possible audience. This financial stability also grants her the creative freedom to experiment and take risks, key components of artistic growth and innovation.

The strategic advantages of building a dedicated audience for co-creation are manifold. Instant feedback from a trusted community can guide product development, reducing the risk associated with launching new offerings. This model encourages a shift from creating for a faceless mass market to engaging with a known community, enabling more targeted and effective innovation. Furthermore, a dedicated fanbase can provide a buffer against market fluctuations, offering a more stable and predictable source of income.

Reflective questions to consider when aiming to cultivate and engage with a dedicated audience include:

1. How can I identify and cultivate a core group of dedicated fans who are genuinely interested in my work and willing to support it financially?
2. What strategies can I employ to foster a deeper connection with my audience, encouraging their active participation and feedback in the creative process?

3. In what innovative ways can I utilise digital platforms to offer exclusive content or experiences that enhance the value of my work for my dedicated fans?
4. How can I leverage the insights and feedback from my dedicated audience to refine and improve my offerings, ensuring they remain relevant and appealing?
5. What measures can I put in place to sustain and grow my dedicated fan base over time, ensuring the long-term viability of my creative or entrepreneurial endeavours?

By addressing these questions, creators and entrepreneurs can develop a more nuanced understanding of audience engagement and the critical role a dedicated fanbase plays in achieving sustainable success. This approach not only enhances the creator-audience relationship but also paves the way for more personalised and impactful creative endeavours.

Global Amplifier 23. Embrace Diversity Of Thought And Culture To Lead Globally

"Strength lies in differences, not in similarities." – Stephen R. Covey

Embracing diversity of thought and culture is increasingly recognised as a cornerstone for successful global leadership and innovation. It involves actively seeking and appreciating the unique insights and perspectives brought by individuals from varied backgrounds, experiences, and cultures. This commitment to diversity is not only ethically sound but also serves as a catalyst for creativity, enabling organisations to devise more comprehensive, inclusive, and effective solutions that resonate on a global scale.

The importance of fostering diversity becomes even more apparent in a globalised economy, where understanding and connecting with diverse markets is crucial. Organisations that fail to embrace diversity risk developing a myopic view of the world, potentially overlooking the nuanced needs of different populations and stifling innovation.

Tech companies like Slack and Zoom stand as shining examples of how multicultural teams can drive innovation and create products that resonate on a global scale. Their platforms, which facilitate communication and collaboration across diverse geographical and cultural boundaries, are a testament to the power of including varied perspectives in the development process. By incorporating team members from different cultural backgrounds, these companies have been able to design features and user interfaces that are intuitive and accessible to a wide range of users. This diversity within their teams has enabled them to preemptively address potential usability issues and incorporate a broad spectrum of user needs and preferences, making their platforms indispensable tools in today's globalised workplace.

In literature, Chimamanda Ngozi Adichie's works, such as "Americanah," offer readers a window into the complexities of identity, migration, and the intersection of cultures. Adichie's narratives, rooted in her own experiences and observations, challenge readers to consider perspectives beyond their own, promoting a deeper understanding and empathy across cultural divides. Her storytelling not only captivates but also educates, bridging gaps between disparate experiences and fostering a global dialogue on important social issues. By bringing diverse voices to the forefront, Adichie illustrates the enriching effect that different cultural perspectives can have on the literary landscape, encouraging readers to embrace a more inclusive view of the world.

Zaha Hadid's architectural legacy is another profound example of how diversity of thought and culture can lead to groundbreaking innovations. Hadid, with her unique vision and refusal to conform to traditional architectural norms, introduced designs that were both futuristic and deeply influenced by her multicultural background. Her work, characterised by flowing, dynamic forms and an avant-garde approach to space, has redefined what is possible in architecture, inspiring a generation of architects to think more creatively and boldly. Hadid's buildings, such as the London Aquatics Centre and the Heydar Aliyev Centre in Baku, stand as iconic symbols of the transformative power of embracing and integrating diverse cultural influences into one's work.

By integrating diversity of thought and culture into all aspects of work, leaders and organisations can unlock new levels of creativity and innovation, ensuring that their offerings are more inclusive, effective, and appealing to a global audience. This inclusive approach not only enhances the relevance and impact of solutions but also positions organisations as leaders in fostering a more connected and understanding world.

Reflective questions to consider include:

1. How can I create an environment within my organisation or team that encourages the expression and integration of diverse perspectives?
2. What strategies can be employed to ensure that decision-making processes within my organisation are influenced by a broad range of cultural insights and viewpoints?
3. How can engaging with and understanding diverse cultures lead to the development of products or services that better cater to global markets?
4. What measures can I take to continually educate myself and my team on the importance of diversity and inclusion, and how can we implement this understanding in our daily operations?
5. In what ways can I leverage diversity to foster innovation and creativity within my field, drawing inspiration from examples like Slack, Zoom, Chimamanda Ngozi Adichie, and Zaha Hadid?

Addressing these questions is essential for leaders and organisations aiming to excel in a globally interconnected landscape, where embracing diversity is key to unlocking creativity, fostering innovation, and achieving sustainable success.

Global Amplifier 24. Ask: What If You Were The Globally Dominant Player?

"To be yourself in a world that is constantly trying to make you something else is the greatest accomplishment." – Ralph Waldo Emerson

Imagining yourself as a globally dominant player in your field opens up a landscape of possibilities and challenges you to elevate your ambitions and agency. This exercise is not about harbouring a desire for power but about envisioning the potential to lead and innovate in a way that addresses global issues and unmet needs effectively

Malala Yousafzai's journey from a young girl in the Swat Valley of Pakistan to a global advocate for girls' education epitomises the profound impact that individual agency and focused ambition can have on the world stage. Her story is a testament to the power of courage, resilience, and a steadfast commitment to a cause in the face of adversity. At a young age, Malala began advocating for girls' rights to education in her community, a stance that brought her into direct conflict with the Taliban. Despite an assassination attempt on her life at just 15 years old, Malala's resolve only strengthened.

Her recovery and subsequent global advocacy work have made her a symbol of resistance against the suppression of children and young people and the right of all children to education. Malala's efforts have significantly raised global awareness about the challenges girls face in accessing education and have mobilised international action. Her work has contributed to policy changes, increased funding, and the establishment of educational programmes worldwide aimed at closing the gender gap in education.

Malala's influence extends beyond her advocacy work; she embodies the idea that young people, regardless of their background, can drive meaningful change. Her story encourages others to take action within their capacities and contexts, demonstrating that focused ambition and a clear vision can indeed lead to substantial global influence and change. Malala's receipt of the Nobel Peace Prize, alongside Kailash Satyarthi, underscores her significant contributions to the fight for children's rights to education.

This visionary mindset pushes you to think beyond local or even national success, encouraging a global perspective in your planning, strategy, and actions. It challenges the conventional, often self-imposed limitations on what you can achieve and inspires a shift towards setting loftier, more impactful goals. By considering the potential to become a globally dominant force in your field, you are prompted to strategise not just for incremental improvements but for major, transformative breakthroughs.

However, reaching such heights of global influence requires more than just ambition; it necessitates a deliberate cultivation of agency through strategic planning, continuous learning, and leveraging technology to connect and engage with a worldwide audience. It also involves building a supportive network that shares your vision and amplifies your message across cultures and continents.

Reflective questions to explore this concept further include:

1. In what specific ways can envisioning global dominance in my field shift my current approach to goal setting and strategic planning?
2. How can I proactively expand my understanding and appreciation of global challenges and opportunities related to my area of expertise?

3. What actions can I take to build and engage with a network that supports my vision for global influence and impact?
4. Which digital tools and platforms are most effective for amplifying my ideas and work on a global scale, and how can I best utilise them?
5. How can I ensure that my efforts to achieve global dominance are aligned with ethical principles and contribute positively to addressing worldwide problems?

By contemplating these questions, you can begin to chart a course towards not only imagining but actively pursuing a role as a global leader in your field. This ambitious vision serves as a powerful motivator, urging you to expand your horizons, embrace innovation, and take meaningful steps towards making a significant global impact.

End of Section Summary: Collective Success and Community

The "Together" section highlights the significant impact of collective ambition, collaboration, and community on achieving success beyond individual capabilities. It underscores the transformative potential of aligning with others, whether through challenging established norms with established powers or forging new partnerships that push the boundaries of innovation. This section emphasises that monumental achievements are often the result of strategic alliances and shared visions, highlighting the importance of collective effort in turning ambitious goals into reality.

Key insights from this section include:

The Power of Moonshots: Inspired by the extraordinary ambition behind the Apollo missions, aiming for the moon symbolises the importance of setting and striving for audacious goals. This approach drives innovation and breakthroughs, as seen in the stories of Fauja Singh and Erin Brockovich, who achieved remarkable feats by challenging perceived limits and pushing beyond conventional expectations.

Redefining Success: By questioning and navigating around established powers and intermediaries, figures like Stella McCartney and Amanda Hocking demonstrate the value of pioneering new paths to success. Their journeys highlight the potential for innovation and independence in redefining market norms and achieving success through direct engagement with audiences or consumers.

Leveraging Technology for Global Reach: The exploration of digital tools and AI in connecting and collaborating globally showcases the pivotal role of technology in expanding the impact and reach of initiatives. It points to the necessity of embracing digital advancements to facilitate global partnerships, enhance learning, and drive forward-thinking strategies across various sectors.

Diversity as a Catalyst for Innovation: The section also emphasises the significance of embracing diversity of thought and culture for global leadership. By highlighting examples from tech companies like Slack and Zoom, and visionaries like Chimamanda Ngozi Adichie and Zaha Hadid, it illustrates how diverse perspectives can foster creativity, lead to more inclusive solutions, and enhance global competitiveness.

Global Dominance Through Visionary Leadership: Imagining oneself as a globally dominant player, as demonstrated by Malala Yousafzai's advocacy for girls' education, serves as a call to action for aspiring leaders to envision and pursue transformative global impacts. It encourages a strategic and expansive approach to leadership that seeks to address global challenges and inspire collective action towards meaningful change.

Reflective questions to further internalise the insights from this section include:

1. How can I more effectively collaborate with others to amplify the impact of my work on a global scale?
2. In what ways can I challenge existing paradigms and forge new pathways to success that are more aligned with contemporary values and technologies?
3. How can I leverage my network and strategic partnerships to achieve goals that were once considered unattainable?

4. What steps can I take to ensure that my strategies for global dominance are inclusive, ethical, and contribute positively to the world?

By engaging with these themes, individuals and organisations are encouraged to look beyond their immediate surroundings and consider the broader implications of their actions. The "Together" section serves as a reminder of the strength found in unity and the potential for collective efforts to achieve unprecedented success, urging readers to embrace collaboration, diversity, and visionary leadership in their pursuit of global influence and impact.

CONCLUSION

In a world characterised by rapid technological advancements and increasing interconnectedness, the pursuit of success demands more than just individual excellence; it requires a holistic understanding of the global landscape, strategic foresight, and a commitment to collective achievement. This book delves into the essence of ambition, the power of agency, the transformative potential of technology, and the unparalleled strength of community and collaboration in achieving global success. Through a series of insights, examples, and reflective questions, it provides a roadmap for individuals and organisations aspiring to make a significant impact on the world stage.

Personal Ambition and Identity

The journey to global influence begins with a deep introspection into one's ambition and identity, emphasising the importance of defining success on one's own terms. By examining the stories of trailblazers like Sara Blakely and Richard Branson, who carved unique paths to success by adhering to their personal visions rather than conforming to external expectations, the book highlights the power of self-defined ambition. It challenges readers to consider their unique strengths and passions, urging them to set goals that not only aspire to achieve greatness but also to exceed the ordinary and embrace innovation.

External Influences and Market Position

As we pivot our gaze outward, the book explores the dynamics of operating within a global ecosystem, emphasising the importance of surpassing the limits set by others and leveraging unmet needs for commercial opportunities. The success stories of Muhammad Yunus's Grameen Bank and d.light demonstrate how addressing specific, global challenges can lead to significant impact and commercial success. This section encourages a data-driven approach to understanding global problems and highlights the importance of innovation and adaptability in redefining industry standards and contributing to global progress.

Enabling Technology

Technology's role as a catalyst for expanding reach and amplifying impact cannot be overstated. Through the exploration of digital tools and platforms, the book showcases how innovations like telemedicine, GitHub, and digital marketing technologies have revolutionised industries by making services more accessible and fostering global collaboration. It underscores the necessity of embracing digital advancements to remain competitive and relevant in the modern landscape, pushing readers to think about how they can harness technology to enhance their global reach and operational efficiency.

Collective Success and Community

The final section of the book, "Together," encapsulates the essence of collective ambition and the importance of strategic alliances in achieving global success. It highlights the value of aiming for moonshot goals, as seen in the extraordinary achievements of figures like Fauja Singh and Erin Brockovich, who pushed beyond perceived limits to effect significant change. By challenging established powers and embracing diversity of thought and culture, as embraced by Stella McCartney and Amanda Hocking, this section illustrates how collaboration and community act as force multipliers, turning individual success into collective triumph.

Throughout the book, readers are encouraged to reflect on their journey, aspirations, and the impact they wish to have on the world. It emphasises the importance of a global perspective, urging individuals to consider the broader implications of their actions and to strive for solutions that promote planetary well-being. The book makes it clear that in today's interconnected world, success is not just about individual achievement but about making a positive impact on a global scale.

The narrative weaves together the themes of ambition, agency, technology, and community, presenting them not as separate entities but as interconnected facets of a comprehensive strategy for achieving global success. It challenges readers to break free from traditional paths, to leverage digital tools for broader reach, and to build strategic connections that transcend cultural and geographical boundaries. By showcasing the transformative potential of aiming high, embracing innovation, and fostering diversity, the book serves as a compelling guide for those seeking to leave a lasting legacy in an increasingly complex and interconnected world.

This book is a call to action for aspiring global leaders and innovators. It provides a framework for understanding the complexities of achieving success in a global context and offers insights into how individuals and organisations can navigate these challenges. Through a combination of strategic foresight, a commitment to diversity and collaboration, and the effective use of technology, it outlines how to not only achieve personal and professional goals but also to contribute to the collective progress of humanity. As the world continues to evolve, the principles laid out in this book offer a roadmap for those looking to make a meaningful impact and achieve unparalleled success in the global arena.

RULE THE WORLD

Sophie Krantz's forthcoming book is titled *Rule the World*. It challenges the sceptics of traditional leadership and outdated practices prevalent in today's headlines and boardrooms. This publication is tailored for entrepreneurs and professionals, both established and emerging, who are navigating the digital era in search of a new leadership paradigm.

This book serves as a guide for those aiming to make a significant professional impact yet feel constrained by the prevailing corporate culture or business environment.

It is not intended for those whose leadership style or aspirations are characterised by:

- Unilateral decision-making, ignoring collaborative input.
- Prioritising immediate profits over sustainability.
- Exploiting resources instead of nurturing them.
- Resisting change and innovation to maintain the status quo.
- Valuing financial gain over social and environmental impact.
- Imposing top-down control and limiting team autonomy.
- Operating opaquely, shunning transparency.
- Avoiding risks, which limits innovation.
- Competing aggressively without regard for broader implications.
- Disregarding the importance of cultural diversity and global perspectives.

The book is a blueprint for individuals who:

- Value teamwork and collective insight.
- Seek to create long-term value beyond short-term financial gains.

- Regard the world's resources as a communal legacy to be sustainably managed.
- View change as an opportunity and tradition as a foundation.
- Believe in harmonising business success with societal progress.
- Advocate for empowering leadership across all levels.
- Support transparent and honest communication.
- Recognise risk as essential for innovation.
- Understand that genuine success benefits entire communities.
- Appreciate the advantages brought by diverse cultures and ideas.
- For those ready to abandon the 'command and conquer' approach in favour of a purpose-driven ambition, this book marks the beginning.

Rule The World positions itself as a counterpoint to the traditional, industrial-era leadership model. It is a manifesto for those who recognise and seek to correct the flaws in the current system, advocating for a leadership style attuned to the digital age. If you find resonance in the outdated approaches of unilateral decision-making, short-term focus, exploitation, resistance to change, and lack of transparency, this book aims to challenge and inspire a reevaluation towards a more progressive, disruptive leadership model.

Conversely, if you identify with a new ethos that prioritises collaboration, sustainability, innovation, and inclusivity, you'll find affirmation and guidance for leading in the digital age. This book is for the entrepreneur or professional who aspires not just to succeed in business but to positively impact the world.

Through its chapters, new versions of leadership are explored, meeting individuals who combine ambition with a deep sense of global responsibility. These leaders are unapologetically global in their ambition, striving for impactful breakthroughs and employing a global perspective to tackle complex challenges and create sustainable, far-reaching solutions.

Sophie Krantz is an influential author and global strategist, renowned for her advocacy of transformative leadership in the digital age. With a career that spans continents and industries, Sophie has devoted herself to empowering leaders and organisations to think bigger and act globally. Her book, "Global Amplifiers: Strategies to Think and Act Bigger in a Changing World," reflects her vision for leadership that leverages global connectivity to drive significant change.

Sophie's initial experiences in multinational corporations and at the International Trade Centre (joint agency of the United Nations and World Trade Organisation) exposed her to the potential for transformative leadership to foster more inclusive and expansive business practices, leading her to explore strategies that enable organisations to scale their impact on a global stage.

Sophie's expertise in Exponential Organizations (ExOs) has made her a sought-after consultant and speaker, celebrated for her ability to lead teams through innovation sprints and strategic design programmes. Her efforts have helped businesses navigate the rapid changes in the global market and inspired them to pursue ambitious, world-altering goals.

Having managing international strategies in over 20 countries, Sophie challenges conventional norms of leadership through her work, promoting a proactive embrace of digital tools and cross-cultural collaboration. She is a prominent figure at global strategy conferences and a mentor to emerging leaders aiming to make a substantial impact in their fields. Her insights on the role of technology and innovation in achieving sustainable and scalable success are frequently featured in international business forums.

Based in Melbourne, Australia, Sophie continues to engage with topics related to leadership, global strategy, and the future of work. She remains committed to her mission of inspiring leaders to explore beyond their boundaries and to use their influence to foster a more equitable and prosperous world.

Sophie facilitates global strategy workshops, executive immersive visits to the world's most most innovative cities, and global mastermind groups for established and emerging leaders. For more information, visit www.sophiekrantz.com.

www.ingramcontent.com/pod-product-compliance
Lightning Source LLC
Chambersburg PA
CBHW040927210326
41597CB00030B/5213